GOOD ✦ OLD ✦ DAYS®

Live It Again™

1953

Prins

Dear Friends,

We had much to celebrate in 1953! For some occasions, like the birthday of our country, we rejoiced with fireworks that lit the sky with bright explosions of color. We celebrated the inauguration of a new president, welcoming Dwight D. Eisenhower with salutes and well wishes, ceremonies and a grand ball. We celebrated with Senator John F. Kennedy and Jacqueline Bouvier on the day of their union as husband and wife in what the press dubbed "the wedding of the year."

The Korean War drew to a conclusion amid cheers and tears as those who served our country returned to American soil. A royal fireworks display was the finale of the coronation of Queen Elizabeth II of England, a regal party we followed in the United States via telecast. Yes, it was a first-rate year in the United States, not only for those headline-worthy special events, but also for the joys of everyday life.

It was a first-rate year, not only for those headline-worthy events, but also for the joys of everyday life.

One of our favorite leisure activities was an evening at the cinema. Whether we chose to go to a theater or headed to the drive-in for the showing, we munched on popcorn, sipped sodas and had a ball with friends and family. Turn to page 6 for a list of the best movies of the year. Yes, we enjoyed movies and also celebrity-watching in general. We adored the mellow voice of Bing Crosby, who is featured on pages 12 and 13.

In television, *I Love Lucy* soared to new heights as Lucille Ball's real-life pregnancy was written into the story line of the television show. *TV Guide* debuted this year with a color photo of baby Desi on the cover—both newborns in 1953.

What about Elvis Presley, our future heartthrob? Within the pages of this book—we'll let the location be a surprise—is a photo of the "king of rock 'n' roll" at his high school prom. It was certainly cause for celebration the day Elvis learned to dance! Join us in remembering a great year through the vivid images and words of *Live It Again 1953*.

REPRINTED WITH PERMISSION OF EXXON MOBIL CORP.

Contents

REPRINTED WITH PERMISSION FROM GENERAL MOTORS CO.

REPRINTED WITH THE PERMISSION OF CARRIER CORP.

TONI FRISSELL / JOHN F. KENNEDY PRESIDENTIAL LIBRARY AND MUSEUM, BOSTON. PUBLIC DOMAIN

1953 Quiz

1. What hit song included a dog's bark and was sung by Patti Page?

2. Who was the first woman to shatter the sound barrier?

3. What TV show promoted Arthur Murray Dance Studios?

4. How many precious jewels adorned the crown worn by Queen Elizabeth II during her coronation on June 2, 1953?

5. What 1953 movie did Marilyn Monroe and Jane Russell star in?

6. What puppet TV show was broadcast in color for the first time on Aug. 30, 1953?

7. What was the No. 1 TV show in 1953?

8. What famous couple wed on Sept. 12, 1953?

Answers are found in this book and on page 127

Best Movies of 1953

A number of exceptional movies came to theaters in 1953, making for an exciting Academy Awards ceremony. The film *From Here to Eternity* won eight Oscars, including Best Supporting Actor for Frank Sinatra, Best Supporting Actress for Donna Reed and Best Director for Fred Zinnemann. *Gentlemen Prefer Blondes* was a lighthearted comedy that starred Marilyn Monroe and Jane Russell in their prime. Audrey Hepburn shone in her role as a sheltered princess in *Roman Holiday*.

Walt Disney Studios continued its tradition of creating feature-length animations from children's classics with *Peter Pan*, a retelling of J. M. Barrie's story. In the movie, Wendy and her brothers experience adventures when Peter Pan, hero of their stories, whisks them away to the magical world of Never Land. The *Peter Pan* characters became firmly connected to The Walt Disney Co. Tiny fairy Tinker Bell became a Disney icon second only to Mickey Mouse. *Peter Pan* was the No. 1 movie of the year.

Montgomery Clift, Donna Reed and Frank Sinatra star in *From Here to Eternity*. The movie was set in 1941 Hawaii and combined the army, boxing and a love affair into a blockbuster movie.

MEMORABLE QUOTE

"Being a sex symbol is a heavy load to carry, especially when one is tired, hurt and bewildered."
—Marilyn Monroe

Audrey Hepburn, winner of the Best Actress award for her role in *Roman Holiday*, is delighted to receive an Oscar from William Holden, who won Best Actor for *Stalag 17*.

Marilyn Monroe and Jane Russell star in *Gentlemen Prefer Blondes*. They are lounge singers on a cruise, enjoying the company of any eligible men they meet.

Chick Daniels, above, composed the song *Lei Aloha*. Arthur Godfrey heard it and asked him to appear on the Godfrey television and radio shows.

Hollywood stars, Elaine Stewart and Shelley Winters playfully pose for the camera. Elaine played the role of Julie Mollison in *Take the High Ground*. Shelley had the lead role of Nancy in *My Man and I*.

Stars Spike Jones, Gale Storm, Vic Damone, Milton Berle, Anna Maria Alberghetti, Herb Shriner and Red Skelton relax poolside at Brynie Foy's ranch.

Actress Rita Moreno's makeup is enhanced while on the set of the movie *El Alaméin*. Rita was from Puerto Rico and broke new ground for Hispanics in the entertainment field.

Celebrities We Admired

How we loved catching a glimpse of celebrities as they went about their daily routines. Noteworthy in 1953 were such greats as multimedia star Bing Crosby, a leader in record sales, radio ratings and motion picture grosses, and Marlon Brando, who became one of the greatest actors of all time. Musician and composer Chick Daniels from Hawaii was occasionally seen on a beach playing his ukulele. Actress Elaine Stewart's striking and shapely beauty attracted attention wherever she went.

Writer Bill Morrow, singer Rosemary Clooney, comedian Bob Hope, and actor and singer Bing Crosby relax after a radio-show rehearsal.

Actors Fernando Lamas and Rhonda Fleming are interviewed by a secretary from Paramount's publicity department.

Handsome actor and heartthrob Marlon Brando is seen while traveling to New York. In 1953, he starred in the movie *Julius Caesar*, making $125,000 per movie.

Celebrities We Admired

Family life

Celebrities' families were equally interesting to fans in the 1950s. In addition to his career as an entertainer, Jerry Lewis was later involved in the fight against muscular dystrophy, hosting an annual telethon. His zest for life included his family. Boxer Tommy Collins was known in the 1950s for his powerful punch. He knocked out 70 percent of his opponents, yet enjoyed time with his wife and baby.

Comedian and actor Jerry Lewis poses with his wife, Patti, and sons Ron, left, and Gary, right, who later became the front man of the 1960s rock group, Gary Lewis & the Playboys.

Walt Disney and his daughters, Sharon and Diane, relax at their Holmby Hills, Calif., home. Disney's worldwide popularity was based on his creativity, imagination and self-made success story.

Audie Murphy was a war hero who later became a big-money Hollywood star and found some success as a country music composer. He gave away all his military medals to his kids. He wanted to forget about the war and concentrate on raising his young son.

Comedian Sid Caesar and his family spent almost every evening at home, watching TV to assess his competition. Caesar pioneered the television variety show format with *Your Show of Shows*, which aired from 1950 until 1954.

Boxer Tommy Collins and wife May are shown with their young son. Collins once won a fight in the fifth round after promising sportswriters he would be home in time for the baby's eleven-o'clock feeding.

Superstars of 1953

Match the celebrity with the role played and TV show they starred in.

1. Vivian Vance
2. Jack Webb
3. William Bendix
4. Richard Crenna
5. Jay Silverheels
6. Jim Backus

A. Walter Denton of *Our Miss Brooks*
B. Judge Bradley Stevens of *I Married Joan*
C. Ethel Mertz of *I Love Lucy*
D. Chester Riley of *The Life of Riley*
E. Sgt. Joe Friday of *Dragnet*
F. Tonto of *The Long Ranger*

Answers: 1-C; 2-E; 3-D; 4-A; 5-F; 6-B

Bing Crosby and his sons Philip, Gary, Dennis and Lindsay enjoy each other's company at Hayden Lake, Idaho. After a summer of hard work on a Nevada ranch, the boys were rewarded with the Idaho vacation.

1953 Trivia

Q. Which 1953 movie did Bing Crosby play a war correspondent stationed in Paris during World War II?

A. Little Boy Lost

Bing comments on Bob Hope's golf game with a playfully disrespectful gesture. They met in the 1930s and remained close friends.

Crosby, rarely seen without a hat, hosted parties with live musical entertainment such as guitarist Perry Botkin and other jazz musicians.

Bing Crosby— The Boo-Boo-Boo Crooner

Bing Crosby was born on May 3, 1903, in Tacoma, Wash. He began singing while studying law at college. He made a name for himself on radio and with records, but singing 16 hours a day took a toll on his voice in 1931. When a doctor warned him he might not sing again, he took a brief respite until his famous voice returned. Bing's mellow, relaxed singing style inspired two generations of pop singers and made him a very successful entertainer. He was also one of Hollywood's top box-office attractions. A sports fan, he died on Oct. 14, 1977, on a golf course.

Bing Crosby had the right voice at the right time. By 1930, sound was being added to movies and most American homes had radios.

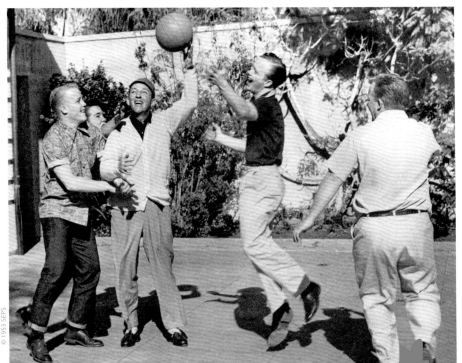

Bing and his sports-minded sons unwind with a pick-up game of basketball. Crosby was a strict disciplinarian at home. He said, "I'm going to demand that they have a goal in life."

Bing Crosby toured Europe with the USO during World War II. As part of the entertainment, GIs in France "capture" him.

Featured Cover Artist, Stevan Dohanos

Artist Stevan Dohanos was born in Lorain, Ohio. With encouragement from family and friends, he chose art as his career and attended the Cleveland Art School. His artwork indicated his interest in the simple pleasures of life. He submitted some of his work to *The Saturday Evening Post*, and his first cover was for the March 7, 1942 issue, depicting anti-aircraft of World War II. He became a regularly featured artist for *The Post*, painting over 100 covers. He died in 1994 at age 87, leaving behind an artistic legacy of the era.

The Metro Daily News

FINAL EDITION

JANUARY 20, 1953

DWIGHT D. EISENHOWER IS INAUGURATED AS THE 34TH PRESIDENT IN WASHINGTON, D.C.

Stevan Dohanos painted eight covers for *The Saturday Evening Post* in 1953. These illustrations are shown here and on the facing page.

What Made Us Laugh

"Say, just how long has she been in there?"

"I've really been impossible today!"

"Good cold shower this morning will have me awake in no time."

"Would you mind moving to the center of the float?"

"You want to see a cute hat over in Section A?"

"Hello, dear. How was your Tuesday Afternoon Discussion Group?"

"I guess it wasn't a shark after all."

"It's high time you had a talk with those new neighbors."

Make Hollywood's favorite
famous Brown Derby Black Bottom Pie

with KNOX the real Gelatine and Baker's Premium No.1 Chocolate

BROWN DERBY BLACK BOTTOM PIE

1 envelope Knox Gelatine
¾ cup sugar
⅛ teaspoon salt
1 egg yolk, slightly beaten
¾ cup milk
4 squares Baker's Unsweetened Chocolate
1 cup **icy cold** evaporated milk, whipped
1 teaspoon vanilla
1 baked 9-inch pie shell
1 cup cream, whipped and sweetened

Mix gelatine, sugar, and salt in top of double boiler. Combine egg yolk and milk and add to gelatine mixture. Add 3 squares of the chocolate. Cook over boiling water until chocolate is melted, stirring often. Remove from heat and beat with egg beater until smooth. Chill until thickened. Then fold in whipped evaporated milk and vanilla. Pile into pie shell and chill. Spread with whipped cream. Shave remaining 1 square chocolate into long curls with vegetable slicer. Sprinkle over pie and stick widest curls upright.

Adapted from the "Brown Derby Cookbook" for use in your kitchen.

Charles Knox developed the world's first pre-granulated gelatin in 1890. As the product gained popularity with homemakers, it revolutionized gel cookery.

"**I GUARANTEE:** A perfect cake every time you bake...cake...after cake ...after cake"

Betty Crocker

"Let's have a pink party… it's so easy with my White Cake mix."

Betty Crocker CAKE MIXES

Beginning in 1921, the Betty Crocker name symbolized General Mills' tradition of service. Though Betty Crocker was not a real person, the image represented quality. The first cake mixes were pioneered in the late 1920s by O. Duff and Sons, but there were problems with packaging and spoiling. In 1947, after four years of research and development, General Mills introduced Betty Crocker's Ginger Cake mix.

Remember Mother with a →

Whitman's Sampler

ALL WHITMAN'S PACKAGES SPECIALLY DECORATED FOR MOTHER'S DAY

A WOMAN NEVER FORGETS THE MAN WHO REMEMBERS

In 1842, Stephen F. Whitman set up a small candy shop in Philadelphia. Whitman knew presentation could be as important as taste, so he created beautiful packaging for his candy. Whitman's became a familiar name from the ads that appeared in newspapers and magazines.

Enduring, Trusted Products

A trip to today's grocery store and a stroll down the aisles will reveal many products that have been mainstays in kitchens throughout America for decades. The stories behind the enduring products pictured here are fascinating. For example, what year was the first bottle of Hires Root Beer sold? It was introduced to the public at the 1876 Philadelphia Centennial Exhibition. The items featured here symbolize a tradition of service to customers.

Charles Hires discovered a recipe for a delicious herbal tea and added it to carbonated soda water to create the first version of Hires Root Beer.

Campbell's, first known as Joseph Campbell & Co., was founded in 1869. The condensed soups that were sold laid the foundation for the giant food company. The first soup sold was Campbell's Tomato Soup.

Better FOR COOKING!

• Cereals, sauces, puddings and any number of other dishes have stepped-up energy—new flavor lure—when you add Sun-Maid Raisins! Rich in calcium, phosphorus and iron, Sun-Maid Raisins are always reliably fresh and wholesome!

Recipe RAISIN SAUCE FOR HAM

• Simmer 1 cup Sun-Maid Raisins (Seedless Nectars or Seedless) in 2 cups water 15 min. Combine 2 Tbs. cornstarch, 2 Tbs. sugar, ⅛ tsp. salt and 2 Tbs. cold water to make a paste. Add to raisins and heat until thickened. Remove from heat. Add 1 Tbs. butter or margarine and 2 Tbs. lemon juice. Mix well. Serve over hot baked ham, ham loaf or any desired meat—for extra flavor and distinction.

Better FOR EATING!

• Healthful Sun-Maid Raisins are the perfect between-meals snack when the youngsters want sweets! Get the Sun-Maid Thrift-I-Pak—six handy pocket packs of raisins at a money-saving low price!

One of the uninvited...

or the life of *the party?*

One of the worst things about bad breath is that you seldom know you have it. Why, even your best friend isn't comfortable telling you. Trust Listerine!

LISTERINE STOPS BAD BREATH
4 times better than chlorophyll or tooth paste

Enduring, Trusted Products

The short, catchy advertising phrases used to lure us to buy products still ring in our heads. One of the most famous slogans was "Good to the last drop!" To coffee drinkers, the saying meant good coffee—Maxwell House Coffee. Campbell Soup Co.'s slogan was "M'm! M'm! Good!" and was first used in 1931 in radio advertising. M&M's were introduced to American GIs serving in World War II along with the phrase, "Melts in your mouth, not in your hands."

He deserves the best
So—have him REACH for a *Remington*

Slogan Quiz

Match the slogan with its brand or product name.

1. "Sometimes you feel like a nut, sometimes you don't."
2. "Breakfast of Champions"
3. "A little dab'll do ya!"
4. "A diamond is forever."
5. "Finger lickin' good."
6. "Fast, fast, fast relief."
7. "Dependable as sunrise."

A. Wheaties
B. Kentucky Fried Chicken
C. Anacin
D. De Beers Consolidated
E. Peter Paul Mounds & Almond Joy
F. Brylcreem
G. Coke

Answers: 1-E; 2-A; 3-F; 4-D; 5-B; 6-C; 7-G

Remington electric shavers were safe, easy and fast, and were great Christmas gifts. The first Remington electric shaver was introduced in 1937.

Merry Christmas
Happy Shaving

Remington
60 DeLuxe
ELECTRIC SHAVER

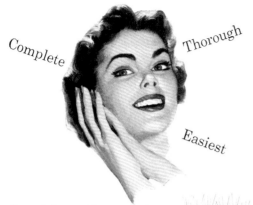

Complete *Thorough*

Easiest

Complete washing and rinsing

Thorough electric drying

Easier loading

You'll be happier with these <u>KitchenAid</u> advantages!

KitchenAid's large wash arm revolves to power wash and double power rinse *each* piece—dishes, glasses, silverware, pots and pans . . . then circulated electric hot air takes over to dry them without leaving unsightly "tear drops." *Your* advantage— bright, sparkling clean dishes!

And the two individual racks slide out conveniently for *easiest* loading . . . you don't "long reach" or lift out racks or hunt space to place your dishes. Another *KitchenAid* advantage— the upper rack adjusts to two positions for extra tall glasses!

Don't *do* the dishes—*have* them done—in a *KitchenAid* Home Dishwasher.

KitchenAid Home Dishwasher Division of **The Hobart Manufacturing Co., Troy, Ohio** In Canada: 175 George Street, Toronto 1

KitchenAid
The Finest Made . . . by

In 1946, KitchenAid introduced a dishwasher for home use that distributed water through a pressurized system.

Whirlpool included many wash-day improvements, such as flexible timing, automatic filling and a fingertip door release.

The Best You Can Buy—

costs no more today . . .

saves more thru the years . . .

Wonderful Whirlpool
AUTOMATIC WASHER

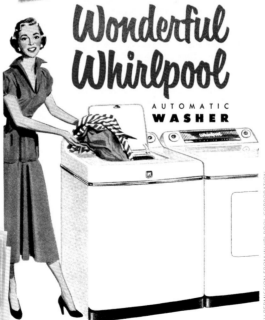

the only automatic washer with
Suds-Miser AND THE *Seven Rinses*

Frankie Laine says:
"HERE'S HOW I GET UP 'On the sunny side of the street'"

WESTINGHOUSE CLOCK RADIO

"For guys who work into the AM hours as I do, that old alarm clock jangle jars like a horn blast in a phone booth. But now with a Westinghouse Clock Radio, waking up is real easy, pleasant as stepping up to a mike. This singing alarm is sensational. It puts you in a sunny mood . . . keeps you on the sunny side of the street all day. There's just nothing like a Westinghouse Clock Radio for starting the day right by waking you to music."

Your Rise and Shine Westinghouse Clock Radio—

Comes in a smart-looking cabinet of durable plastic. Turns itself on automatically . . . added extra alarm for hard-to-wake sleepers. Provides a powerful, dependable radio with finest tone and selectivity. Model 388T5.

ONLY $34.95

At your dealer's (Slightly higher West and South)

YOU CAN BE SURE . . . IF IT'S
Westinghouse

George Westinghouse, founder of the Westinghouse Co., came up with many ideas to make technology better, faster and more efficient. As a result, his company survived him and has lasted for decades.

The Metro Daily News
THE WEATHER
FINAL EDITION
VOLUME 57—No. 161

FEBRUARY 1, 1953

10 PAGES   FIVE CENTS

YOU ARE THERE WITH WALTER CRONKITE DEBUTS ON CBS TELEVISION
The initial telecast is "The Landing of the Hindenburg."

Dancers Marge and Gower Champion kick up their heels at the Coconut Grove in Los Angeles.

Husband and wife dance instructors, Arthur and Kathryn Murray, introduced older viewers to ballroom dancing and also taught many of the popular novelty steps.

Actors Betsy Palmer and James Dean dance together in this still from a 1953 episode of the CBS television show, *Danger*.

We Loved to Dance

Dancing was a natural reaction to the toe-tapping music of 1953. Music was ever present, whether in your head or piped out through radios or record players. Wherever young people connected, there was sure to be some sort to music to get the participants moving. Arthur Murray Dance Studios capitalized on the latest dance crazes and taught such dances as the mambo, the jive and the bunny hop. Arthur and Kathryn Murray's success evolved into a popular TV dance show, *The Arthur Murray Party*, that was a mixture of teaching, exhibition and a way to promote their studios.

Popular dances of 1953 were often energetic, fast-paced and exciting.

Above, Elvis Presley is shown with his 1953 high school prom date. An Elvis Presley who didn't know how to dance? According to his date he was relatively clueless, but it wasn't long until he became a singer known for his moves.

"Wonderful place to dance—too bad there's no music!"

Our Favorite Melodies

One of the top hits of 1953 was the novelty song "The Doggie in the Window," performed by Patti Page. The lyrics were catchy and paired with the occasional bark of a dog. Other chart-makers and heartbreakers of the year were Dean Martin, Tony Bennett and Frank Sinatra. "Your Cheatin' Heart" was written and recorded by country star Hank Williams in 1952, but was not released until after his death in 1953. It is considered to be one of the great songs of country music.

Tony Bennett performs on stage in Cleveland, Ohio, as teenage girls in the audience scream. His warm, husky tenor made him one of the most popular recording artists of the era.

Dean Martin leans against a piano in this 1953 photo. His song, "That's Amore" became a major hit and his signature tune. *Amore* means "love" in Italian.

Les Paul and Mary Ford perform their hit song "Vaya Con Dios" at the Paramount Theatre in New York.

Music Trivia

Q. What is the first line of the song "That's Amore"?

A. "When the moon hits your eye like a big pizza pie, that's amore."

Top Hits of 1953

"That's Amore"
Dean Martin

"The Doggie in the Window"
Patti Page

"Vaya Con Dios"
Les Paul & Mary Ford

"Your Cheatin' Heart"
Hank Williams

"Rags to Riches"
Tony Bennett

"I've Got the World on a String"
Frank Sinatra

"You Belong to Me"
Jo Stafford

"I Believe"
Frankie Laine

"South of the Border"
Frank Sinatra

"Stranger in Paradise"
Tony Bennett

Jo Stafford, admired for the clarity of her voice, was one of the most versatile singers of the time. She had a hit song in 1953 with "You Belong to Me."

The *I Love Lucy* show introduced "audience reaction" to live productions for television. It was the No. 1 show in 1953 and a perennial favorite from 1951 through 1961.

Jack Webb, second from the left, star of the detective show *Dragnet*, confers with Sgt. Vance Brasher, Sgt. Marty Wynn and Capt. Jack Donahoe, the real-life Los Angeles detectives who helped to edit the show seen on Thursdays at 9 p.m. in 1953.

Tops on Television

I Love Lucy
CBS

Dragnet
NBC

Arthur Godfrey's Talent Scouts
CBS

You Bet Your Life
NBC

The Milton Berle Show
NBC

Arthur Godfrey and His Friends
CBS

Ford Theatre
NBC

The Jackie Gleason Show
CBS

Fireside Theater
NBC

This Is Your Life
NBC

Television's Golden Age

Television was booming in 1953. Hollywood was busy producing more than twice as many hours of television as it was for movies. New studios sprang up seemingly overnight to meet the increased needs of an industry that television spokesmen referred to as the "young giant." A number of shows such as *Our Miss Brooks* originated on radio and were heard throughout the 1950s on both radio and television media.

The June Taylor Dancers appeared on *The Jackie Gleason Show* that aired on and off from 1952 until 1970. The variety hour was produced live from New York and later from Miami Beach.

This Is Your Life was a TV show that surprised unsuspecting individuals with their life stories.

During a taping of *Our Miss Brooks*, actress Eve Arden, as Miss Brooks, adjusts a dress on actor Robert Rockwell. The cast members looking on at far left are Richard Crenna and Gloria McMillan.

Television's Golden Age

Shows introduced in 1953

As television grew more popular the number of shows increased, especially those created with children in mind. *Romper Room* was introduced and aired until 1991. *Time* magazine wrote that it was "the world's largest classroom." In 1953, *Winky Dink and You* aired on Saturdays at 11 a.m. It was likely the first example of "interactive" television. The show starred a cartoon boy named Winky Dink.

Danny Thomas starred in *Make Room for Daddy*, on Tuesdays at 9 p.m. in 1953. The show was later changed to *The Danny Thomas Show* and had a long life, airing until 1964. The show was an adaptation of Danny's own life and frequent absences due to his career as an entertainer. The title came from a phrase his family used in real life. When Danny returned home, his children shifted bedrooms to "make room for Daddy." The stars of the show were Jean Hagen, Danny Thomas, Rusty Hamer and Sherry Jackson.

LUCY'S $50,000,000 BABY

TV GUIDE

COMPLETE PROGRAM LISTINGS—April 3-9
15¢

DESIDERIO ALBERTO ARNAZ IV

TV GUIDE MAGAZINE COVER COURTESY OF TV GUIDE MAGAZINE, LLC © 1953

TV Guide premiered in April 1953 and became a major source of TV listings and reviews. The first issue covered the birth of Desiderio Alberto Arnaz IV, a television milestone that included Lucille Ball's real life pregnancy in the *I Love Lucy* TV series. It wasn't long until *TV Guide* became America's top-selling weekly magazine.

The children's show *Winky Dink and You* featured a cartoon boy who found himself in dilemmas. To save him, viewers drew required pictures on a special acetate sheet on their TV screens for the show host, Jack Barry, shown on the screen.

Television Shows Debuting in 1953

Judge for Yourself
Jukebox Jury
Make Room for Daddy
Place the Face
Pride of the Family
Romper Room
The Ray Bolger Show
Valiant Lady
Winky Dink and You
You Are There

"What's the use my turning on the charm when the bases are loaded?"

Hostess Susan Gifford of *Romper Room* instructs the children. Between games and activities using *Romper Room* products, kids at home and in the studio received lessons in good behavior.

1953 STROMBERG-CARLSON CO.

"there is nothing finer than a STROMBERG-CARLSON."

The Barry — $850* Model L2593H in lovely Cherry veneers and solids. AM-FM Radio, 24" TV, Cobra-Matic® Record Player.

The Patrician — $489.95* Model L2270H. Provincial. In natural Cherry veneers, solids, 21" screen, 10-inch speaker.

The Saratoga — $399.95* Model L2280R. Traditional. In deep Mahogany veneers, solids. New 21-inch Cinébeam Picture.

The Wellington — $289.95* Model L2235E. Modern. In bleached Mahogany veneer, 21-inch screen, new Band Shell Speaker.

*Manufacturer's suggested retail price. Includes Federal Excise Tax and Parts and Tubes Warranty. Slightly higher in South and Far West.

FOUR OF THE 52 NEW **ZENITHS** PRICES BEGIN AT $179.95*

The stunning new Zeniths featured greater tonal range as a result of the company's advertised engineering leadership. The amplifier and tuner combined with the speaker increased the range of tones heard by 50 percent.

The Imperial television by Stromberg-Carlson boasted the widest viewing angle available and high-quality sound for television, records and radio. The cabinet was made of premium, hand-rubbed mahogany veneers.

Television's Golden Age

Tubes on the market

The television boom continued in 1953, with about 50 percent of Americans now owning a television set. As demand grew, the manufacturers jockeyed for the top spots in the industry. Advertised features in television sets included life-like picture quality, richness of tone and the ability to pull in pictures where other sets failed. Simple table models were available along with more expensive styles that were encased in finely crafted wood cabinets that looked more like furniture. Other companies combined a television, radio and record player into a single entertainment unit.

RCA Victor advertised Rotomatic tuning that screened out static. Just turn one knob—click!—and your station appeared.

ALL-CHANNEL RECEPTION WITH UHF BUILT RIGHT IN NOW! *(This feature is optional.)*

The Crosley television set was advertised as ideal for fringe reception areas with its superior reception.

21-inch Television

$229 95

The new BARTON brings you 21-inch TV for the lowest price in RCA Victor history. Built-in UHF tuning, optional at extra cost. Ebony finish. Matching stand available, extra.

RCA VICTOR than any other television

Tmks. ®   Division of Radio Corporation of America

WORD SCRAMBLE

Unscramble the letters to spell out 1953 television manufacturers.

1. HNZEIT
2. LYSCORE
3. ARC CRTIVO
4. GMBORSTRE-LRSACNO
5. OTNMUD
6. VLISAYAN

A. 1-Zenith; 2-Crosley; 3-RCA Victor; 4-Stromberg-Carlson; 5-DuMont; 6-Sylvania

Radio Stars & Hits of 1953

Amos 'n' Andy

Bing Crosby

The Bob Hope Show

Crime Classics

Dragnet

Fibber McGee and Molly

Gunsmoke

The Lone Ranger

Mr. Keen, Tracer of Lost Persons

The Shadow

Suspense

This Is Your FBI

The Whistler

Yours Truly, Johnny Dollar

We Heard It on the Radio

Though television was fierce competition, radios had one advantage. Compact models could be taken anywhere. The pint-size versions were easy to carry around the house and ideal for tucking into a suitcase when traveling. The Zenith radio at lower left sold for about $36, and the Zenith clock radio shown on the facing page cost about $50. American commercial radio was divided into block programming, with designated times of day for big band, soap opera or chat. Something totally different, the Top 40, began around 1953 and featured rock 'n' roll hits along with lively deejays.

British actor David Niven personified dapper charm. His radio work earned him extra money and kept his name in the forefront of the public's awareness.

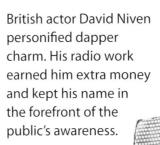

COURTESY OF ZENITH

ZENITH
The royalty of television and RADIO

Bing Crosby rehearses for his radio show with jazz violinist Joe Venuti. Bing starred on various series and hosted an annual *Christmas Sing With Bing* when he always sang his hit "White Christmas."

COURTESY OF ZENITH

The Metro Daily News

FINAL EDITION

MARCH 19, 1953

ACADEMY AWARDS PROGRAM IS TELEVISED FOR THE FIRST TIME

Bob Hope presided as host for the awards. This was also the first ceremony to be held in Hollywood and New York City simultaneously.

HANK BAEB

"That was the 'Anvil Chorus' as played by Spike Jones and the boys …"

MEMORABLE QUOTE

"My first day at the President's Desk. Plenty of worries and difficult problems. But such has been my position for a long time—the result is that this just seems (today) like a continuation of all I've been doing since July '41—even before that!"

—Dwight D. Eisenhower, January 21, 1953

Special inauguration buttons were created for the occasion.

Dwight D. Eisenhower takes the oath of office of the president of the United States.

The inaugural parade was attended by an estimated one million persons. President Eisenhower waves to spectators from a car. The parade included about 50 organization and state floats that cost a total of about $100,000.

President Dwight D. Eisenhower and First Lady Mamie Eisenhower, in the center, are shown at their Inaugural Ball in 1953.

President Eisenhower's Inaugural Year

Dwight D. Eisenhower was sworn into office on January 20, 1953. There had not been a Republican president since Herbert Hoover, who held office from 1929 through 1933. Two Bibles were used at the ceremony—one was from George Washington's inauguration; the other given to Eisenhower by his mother. During his inaugural address, he talked specifically about foreign policy and the need for peace. After his speech, he dashed over to kiss Mamie on the cheek, which the *Los Angeles Times* called "the most public kiss in history."

President Eisenhower witnesses the April 11, 1953, swearing-in ceremony of Oveta Culp Hobby as the first secretary of the U.S. Department of Health, Education and Welfare. President Eisenhower appointed women to a number of prominent posts.

Ike and Mamie Eisenhower are seen on their arrival at the National Airport in Washington, D.C. Mamie Eisenhower was beloved by the public for her charm and wifely devotion.

President Eisenhower, right, shakes hands with Rep. Daniel Reed, the chairman of the House Ways and Means Committee. Vice President Richard M. Nixon, left, was the liaison between the White House and Congress.

This view captures some of the Waco, Texas, tornado damage. The twister struck on a weekday, claiming 114 lives.

News in the Making

U.S. events

Among the newsworthy items of 1953 was President Eisenhower's inaugural ceremony. It was the first such ceremony to be seen on television. The event was viewed live by more people than all other inaugurations combined. The residents of Waco, Texas, thought they were immune to tornadoes until May 11, 1953, when an F5 twister swept through their downtown. The Pentagon approved the testing of an atomic cannon in Nevada named Atomic Annie. The cannon was fired just once, but it was enough for the Soviet Union to take note. Senator Joseph McCarthy continued to search for targets for his anticommunist and disloyalty agenda.

Senator Joseph McCarthy became famous for his investigation into communist activity in the United States.

FAMOUS BIRTHDAYS
Kay Lenz, March 4 actress
Deborah Raffin, March 13 actress (Julie Camden Hastings of *7th Heaven*)

This photo chronicles the first time a nuclear device is fired from a cannon. The resulting fireball was seen at the Nevada Proving Grounds on May 25, 1953.

School students watch the inauguration of President Eisenhower live on television.

News in the Making

World affairs

There was much celebration in England for the coronation of Queen Elizabeth II on June 2, 1953, who actually became queen in 1952 after her father's death. Masses of people gathered in London for the grand event, even though the weather was rainy. When it was disclosed that the coronation would be broadcast on television, the sales of TV sets skyrocketed.

Another celebrated world event in 1953 was the conquering of Mount Everest, the world's highest peak. On May 29, Edmund Hillary and Tenzing Norgay, members of a British Commonwealth team lead by Colonel John Hunt, spent 15 minutes on the summit that Hillary described as a "symmetrical, beautiful snow cone."

Tenzing Norgay reaches the summit of Mount Everest, the world's highest mountain. Why would anyone attempt such a dangerous stunt? "Because it's there," said British climber George Mallory, who died trying.

Soviet leader Joseph Stalin died on March 5, 1953. Stalin led his country to victory over Nazi Germany in World War II. After the war, he installed communist governments in Eastern Europe and pressed for the development of nuclear weapons.

TTY IMAGES

1953 Trivia

Q. What was the weight of the solid-gold crown Queen Elizabeth II wore for her coronation?

A. 4 pounds, 12 ounces

World News

Outstanding Events

Soviet Leader Joseph Stalin Dies

Coronation of Queen
Elizabeth II of England

Mount Everest Conquered

Queen Elizabeth II and Prince Philip can be seen through the windows of the royal carriage as they arrive at Trafalger Square on June 2, 1953. The Queen was crowned at Westminster Abbey in London that day. The coronation came to a dramatic close at midnight when the skies over the River Thames were filled with a spectacular fireworks display. The crown Queen Elizabeth wore is known as St. Edward's Crown, made in 1661 for the coronation of King Charles II, and is set with 444 precious stones.

News in the Making

The medical report

Significant reductions of cavities were reported by dentists in 1953. Though adding fluoride to drinking water was not a new practice, it became an official policy of the U.S. Public Health Service by 1951. New in 1953 was the addition of anti-enzymes in toothpastes that protected teeth from tooth decay acids all day long.

One of the greatest scientific discoveries of the 20th century was James Watson and Francis Crick's cracking of the DNA code, announced in February 1953. This new understanding later helped scientists find cures for disease and prosecutors identify criminals.

On March 26, 1953, Dr. Jonas Salk announced a polio breakthrough. Early trials of his vaccine were successful and he was known across the country as "The Man Who Saved the Children."

American geneticist and biologist Dr. James D. Watson and English scientist Francis Crick worked together to unravel the mystery of DNA. Watson is shown holding a molecular model.

Scientist and physician Jonas Salk smiles while holding aloft two containers of the anti-polio vaccine he developed.

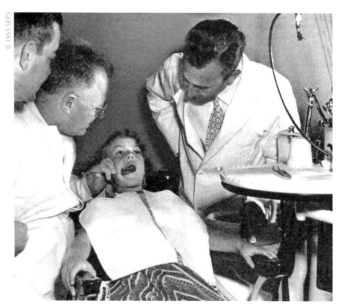

Doctors Dennis Singleton, H.T. Dean and F.A. Arnold check the teeth of a child who had been drinking fluorinated water for eight years.

News in the Making

The Korean War

Dwight D. Eisenhower promised an end to the Korean War during his 1952 presidential campaign. Shortly after taking office, he fulfilled his campaign promise. On July 27, 1953, the peace treaty was signed. The most difficult issue was what to do about the prisoners of war. Many of the North Korean and Chinese prisoners did not want to go home, a great blow to communist pride. Though the loss of human lives was high, there were some positive results of the war. It caused the United States to remain in a higher state of combat readiness and ended discrimination against African-American soldiers. Black and white troops lived and fought side by side.

Since the outbreak of war in Korea, the United States worked to build up its air power. The potent North American AJ Savage had more range than any other carrier-based bomber aircraft.

Korean War veterans return home amid celebrations.

The Metro Daily News

FINAL EDITION

APRIL 10, 1953

HOUSE OF WAX, STARRING VINCENT PRICE, PREMIERES

This is the first horror movie ever to be made in 3-D.

Large Sikorsky helicopters made hill-hopping air-assault tactics possible and gave the U.S. Marines more punch in Korea.

FAMOUS BIRTHDAYS
Ron Clements, April 25 Disney animation director
Merrill Osmond, April 30 actor, singer (Osmond Brothers, Donnie & Marie)

U.S. Army Gen. Mark W. Clark is shown at the signing of the Armistice Agreement that stopped the fighting in Korea.

What Made Us Laugh

"… and then say, 'Dinner is served.' "

"The neighbors have been so kind and understanding—Mr. Beemer got right out and put rock salt on his walk."

"I'm just dying to hear his alibi—last year he blamed it on the Democrats."

"Drove all the way from El Paso—650 miles."

"Got to hand it to the champ—
he really rests between rounds!"

"Say, you two are missing all the fun!"

"Why, Frank, you're trembling."

"Mother, this is Albert, who, I believe, is going to be the
answer to that question you asked me the other day."

1953 Automobiles

Price Sensation of the Year!

$1499.50

Aero-Lark 2-Door Sedan
LIST PRICE
F.O.B. Toledo, Ohio. Plus
Federal Taxes, State and
Local Taxes (if any), Freight
Delivery and Handling
Charges. Optional Equipment, Extra.

Aero + Willys

The body and frame of this Aero Willys car was welded into a strong unit for "bank vault" safety. Six adults could sit comfortably on the five-foot-wide seats.

DOLLAR FOR DOLLAR YOU CAN'T BEAT A

Pontiac

A GENERAL MOTORS MASTERPIECE

First And Foremost—It's Thoroughly Dependable!

The big news from automakers in 1953 was that air conditioning was back and better. Air conditioning had been tried in cars way back in the 1930s. The units were optional, costly and took up half of the entire trunk space. They were also not very efficient without a thermostat or shut-off switch inside the car and were discontinued in the early 1940s. In 1953, Chrysler advertised perfect driving weather year-round with systems with a single knob control. Passengers traveled in comfort with the windows closed, enjoying air that never went stale or built up unpleasant humidity.

Take the Key and See—
You'll Find None so New as **Nash** *Airflyte*

The Nash Ambassador Airflyte, beginning at $2,145, had reclining seats and the widest windshield and rear window ever built into an automobile.

With a 122-inch wheelbase, this Pontiac was designed and built to deliver thousands of carefree miles with only routine maintenance.

Try a 60-Second Ride on this page

WATCH 'EM WATCH YOU... THAT'S UNIFIED DESIGN YOU'RE LOOKING AT

NO TENSION — JUST LIQUID EASINESS   YOU'RE AN ACTION PICTURE IN TECHNICOLOR   RADIANT WITH NEW COLOR AND RICHNESS, ALIVE WITH 1953 POWER.

Then – try a 60-minute ride at your dealer's!

GET THE FACTS — AND YOU'LL GO FOR THE NEW 1953 **MERCURY**

Mercury—symbolizing the progress of Ford Motor Company in its 50th anniversary year.

Mercury advertised smooth performance, the greatest in all of Mercury's V-8 history.

All New '53 Dodge
V-EIGHT OR SIX

According to this advertisement, the sleek and trim new 1953 Dodge took curves like a sports car with a more rigid frame, new stabilizer suspension and lower center of gravity. It sold for $2,245.

1953 Trivia

Q. Which motor company celebrated its 50th anniversary during 1953?

A. Ford Motor Co. was founded on June 16, 1903

Worth more when you buy it... worth more when you sell it!

Ford

The Ford Country Sedan sold for about $2,267 and was powered by the only V-8 engine in the low-price field.

1953 Automobiles

Feeling the breeze

Its beauty is just the beginning

The greatest
BUICK
in 50 great years

Buick's new luxury sports car was the Skylark, priced at $5,000. The car had a V-8 engine, power steering and brakes, and hydraulic control of the windows, top, front seat and radio antenna.

Now–let's drive towards tomorrow **LINCOLN**

Crowning achievement of Ford Motor Company's 50th Anniversary –"50 Years Forward on the American Road"

The new Lincoln offered an unsurpassed choice of colors for the luxurious interiors.

1953 was the first year of production of the Corvette. All the cars had white exteriors and red interiors. Production was limited to 300 total units with a base price of $3,498.

The Oldsmobile Ninety-Eight Convertible coupe was a classic car that sold for $3,229.

"ROCKET" ENGINE
O L D S M O B I L E

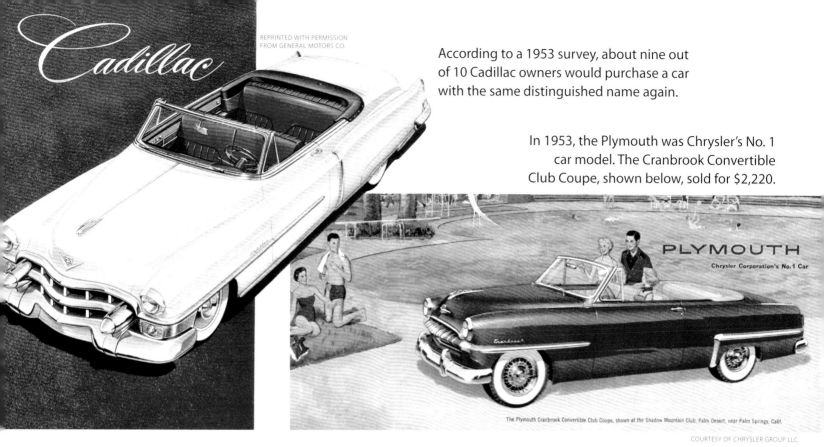

Cadillac

According to a 1953 survey, about nine out of 10 Cadillac owners would purchase a car with the same distinguished name again.

In 1953, the Plymouth was Chrysler's No. 1 car model. The Cranbrook Convertible Club Coupe, shown below, sold for $2,220.

PLYMOUTH

Chrysler Corporation's No. 1 Car

The Plymouth Cranbrook Convertible Club Coupe, shown at the Shadow Mountain Club, Palm Desert, near Palm Springs, Calif.

Why going places is twice the fun and half the work...in a DE SOTO

There was extra room, chair-level seats and a great new view over the hood of a DeSoto.

1953 Automobiles

Experiencing the luxury

Cadillac advertised power and responsiveness along with handling ease and comfort.

REPRINTED WITH PERMISSION FROM GENERAL MOTORS CO.

Cadillac

MAKE A DATE WITH A "ROCKET 8"

OLDSMOBILE

The 1953 Oldsmobile Ninety-Eight Holiday coupe was a youthful, smart hardtop with custom interiors and air conditioning. The base price was $3,022.

The Packard Clipper was built for those who wanted the finest. It was a big car at an intermediate price of $2,745.

America's Most Advanced New Car!

PACKARD

REPRINTED WITH PERMISSION OF STUDEBAKER NATIONAL MUSEUM

LINCOLN

Crowning achievement of Ford Motor Company's 50th Anniversary — "50 Years Forward on the American Road"

REPRINTED WITH PERMISSION FROM FORD MOTOR CO.

Imperial
BY CHRYSLER

Motoring for those who want to forget yesterday

Behind the window glass of a Lincoln was the comfort and beauty of a modern living room. It was the first car that had a 4-way power seat that moved up, down, back and forth.

The Chrysler Imperial limousine, with a base price of $7,044, was the choice for those who could afford any motor car in the world.

The Studebaker Commander V-8 Starliner sold for $2,374. It had the look of a costly foreign car, but was down-to-earth in price.

Styling straight out of the dream book! '53 Studebaker

REPRINTED WITH PERMISSION OF STUDEBAKER NATIONAL MUSEUM

A railroad engineer was in charge of the locomotives as well as the mechanical operation of the train, including speed and handling.

Many farmers in the 1950s raised a variety of livestock instead of concentrating on just one area. More farmers were using tractors as a replacement for the traditional horses or mules.

DANGER

RADIOACTIVE MATERIAL WITHIN

A laboratory technician studies the radioactive material at an atomic energy plant.

One of the most important tasks of the neighborhood pharmacist was compounding prescriptions. The job required extra care, accuracy and a special sense of responsibility.

All in a Day's Work

1953 was a great year to be looking for work. Employment expanded in private, public and self-employment sectors. Housing construction continued to boom along with the many jobs related to that field. Another large job market was the auto industry, with major car companies enjoying huge volumes of orders. Union jobs offered a safe, secure work environment with the possibility for advancement and increasing salary over time. There was an abundance of jobs available in both blue-collar and white-collar sectors. Jobs for engineers and chemists increased right along with the demand for steel and plastics.

Constructing new roads was hard work, but jobs were readily available due to the growth of the United States highway system.

MEMORABLE QUOTE
"The physician can bury his mistakes, but the architect can only advise his client to plant vines—so they should go as far as possible from home to build their first buildings"

—Frank Lloyd Wright

"The grass is always greener …"

All in a Day's Work

Women on the job

Many of the advertisements of 1953 emphasized the stay-at-home wife and mother. Most of society at that time believed a woman's destined roll was to care for her family. The magazines of the day were filled with images of dedicated housewives who were satisfied with meeting their family's needs and shopping for goods to make their chores easier. Yet, as technology shortened the time the tasks required, women had more time to explore other pursuits, finding fulfillment in jobs and volunteer work along with homemaking.

This young lady is graduating from the United Air Lines' stewardess school. No tuition was charged for the program, but only one out of 35 applicants qualified to enter.

Offices were more labor-intensive in the 1950s. Even typing a simple letter could be demanding, because mistakes were difficult to correct.

REPRINTED WITH PERMISSION FROM IBM

The Metro Daily News FINAL EDITION

MAY 18, 1953

JACQUELINE COCHRAN IS THE FIRST WOMAN TO SHATTER THE SOUND BARRIER
She piloted an F-86 Sabre jet at 652 mph over Rogers Dry Lake, Calif.

Mothers and daughters found fulfilling careers as telephone operators. "Mother did all right, and I hope to do as well," said one operator.

The amazingly graceful dancing Rockettes were the precision stylists of Radio City Music Hall in New York.

"Not that far in!"

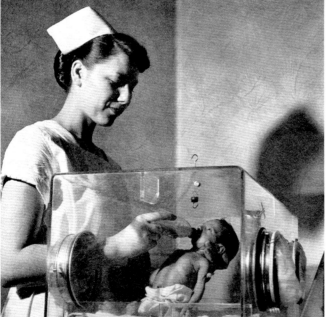

The need for nurses was universal. This nurse nurtures a premature baby.

Women who worked were busy ladies as they combined a career with mothering their children.

Homeowners often painted woodwork and furniture. Paint was inexpensive and easy to keep clean with just soap and water. The traditional living room at left glows with a gold and green color scheme accented with white trim. Bedrooms were roomier than before, and it was possible to have more furniture for storage and for personal convenience, like the dressing table shown above.

This couple is looking for the perfect city apartment. While they check out the closet, their son is much more interested in finding places to play outdoors.

Our Homes

The ranch house remained the dominant American home style. This design combined simple gable roofs with wide eaves, along with open floor plans and large windows. Following the restrictions of World War II, interior designers increased their efforts to create rooms that would meet a variety of customer interests and be down-to-earth ideas homeowners would be proud of. Furniture was made to appeal to both traditional and modern-minded customers. Much of the wood was either cherry or walnut stained dark. Oversized furniture pieces were sold for more comfortable television viewing.

It's moving day, and while the family is busy arranging their new living space, the neighborhood dogs gather around to see the canine newcomer.

Kitchens were cozy and cheerful rooms with the right paint and decorative touches. Bathrooms, such as the one shown on this page, were becoming more attractive as well as utilitarian with the use of pink fixtures.

Imagine! Only
$**69**95
Complete with deluxe tools

New Super-Powered

EUREKA
Roto-Matic SWIVEL-TOP CLEANER

This swivel-top cleaner by Eureka was equipped with adjustable suction so even the sheerest curtains could be vacuumed. The attachments clipped neatly to the side of the unit and were always on hand. There was no dust bag to empty; instead, a large paper bag lifted out and was easily thrown away. No dirt ever touched the hands.

This Servel refrigerator ad boasted to be the first that made ice cubes automatically. It was advertised as the refrigerator marvel of the year.

Our Homes

Time-saving devices

As scientists and engineers returned to civilian life after World War II, the 1950s were filled with an explosion of technological advances that brought amazing new products to consumers. Vacuum cleaners boasted attachments and features that made cleaning the house a breeze. Small appliances of all conceivable types were designed to ease the labor of cooking for a family. Refrigerators became available with that wonderful device, the automatic ice maker.

SERVEL—WORLD'S FIRST AND ONLY REFRIGERATOR THAT—

Makes Ice Cubes Without Trays!

AND PUTS 'EM IN A BASKET ALL AUTOMATICALLY!

STARTS ITSELF! REFILLS ITSELF! STOPS ITSELF!

Servel Refrigerators start as low as $**219**95

Models for every family! Prices for every budget! Sizes from 6 to 11½ cu. ft.

NO TRAYS TO FILL! NO TRAYS TO SPILL! NO TRAYS TO EMPTY! OR FORGET TO REFILL!

SERVEL—THE NAME TO WATCH FOR GREAT ADVANCES IN REFRIGERATION AND AIR CONDITIONING...

The Modern Tap Water Iron!

CASCO
STEAM and DRY IRON

Hamilton Beach branched out into all sorts of kitchen gadgets that made food processing fun and exciting but also rather pricey for 1953.

HAMILTON BEACH **Liqui-Blender** Exciting to give— and to own! New 'Cut-n-Fold' action blends faster, cuts finer—makes meal preparation more fun than work! Blends soups, sauces, cakes— purees vegetables finer than canned baby foods. Liquefies, blends, purees, mixes, chops, grates, pulverizes. 2 speeds. Mason-jar thread. Recipe book. Gives twice the usual cutting power, for just **$37.50**

HAMILTON BEACH **Food Mixer** Compare... then spend dollars less for this mixer that's easiest-to-use! Exclusive Mixguide puts ten tested speeds under your thumb. Bowl Control shifts bowl while beaters revolve. One-hand portability—beater slides on and off stand. Here's long, trouble-free service you can give proudly. Juice extractor sold separately. $4.50*. mixer with two bowls, only **$39.50**

Homemakers had to buy distilled water for their steam irons until Casco introduced a stainless steel model that could be filled from the tap. The iron was lighter for less strain on the wrists and back. It sold for $19.95.

HAMILTON BEACH
Beats everything

Hamilton Beach Co., Division of Scovill Mfg. Co., Racine, Wisconsin

Prices subject to change without notice.

HAMILTON BEACH **Home Drink Mixer** Give family fun... real soda fountain drinks at home! The kids will love making super-duper malteds (the kind you eat with a spoon). And you'll enjoy whipping up tasty fruit drinks, refreshing frozen orange juice, and "fluffing" mixed drinks for better flavor. 16-oz. container delivers two full glasses. 14½" high. Recipe book gives loads of suggestions **$22.50**

HAMILTON BEACH **Mixette** A work-saver that's sure to please—and it's under twenty dollars! Hamilton Beach quality and more big-mixer features make Mixette America's most popular portable. Beats, mixes, mashes, whips—in any bowl or pan. One-hand operation; 3 speeds under your thumb. Stands on end for draining batter, hangs on wall for storage. Beaters snap out for cleaning. In gift box **$19.75**

NOW! A deluxe ¾hp. Air Conditioner at a ½hp. price!

The stunning new

Servel ELECTRIC

AIR CONDITIONER

Servel's stunning Room Air Conditioners in Mahogany or Blond finishes, with ivory grilles and anodized gold trim—to match any color scheme!

NEW! EXCLUSIVE 1-DIAL CONTROL! At last—an air conditioner that's *simple* to operate! No tricky double dials—it's automatic! Just set dial to 1) full-power cooling, 2) night cooling, 3) outdoor air mixed with cool, 4) fresh air circulation, 5) stale air exhaust.

NEW! 50% MORE COOLING POWER at no extra cost! Servel's ¾ H.P. model costs you no more than ordinary ½ H.P. air conditioner! Keeps you cool on hottest days, when undersize units fail! See Servel's new 1 H.P. model too!

NEW! SUPER-QUIET COOLING SYSTEM! Sound-absorbing cushion, plus extra sound insulating wall, keep Servel quiet as a whisper!

NEW! AUTOMATIC TEMPERATURE REGULATOR! Servel's built-in thermostat keeps room at even temperature! Never over or under-cools! Optional on ¾ H.P. model—standard on 1 H.P. model.

NO-DRAFT GRILLES! Adjustable grilles keep your room uniformly cool—prevent chilly drafts!

5-YEAR WARRANTY on Servel's hermetically sealed cooling system! AC only.

3/4 H.P. model in Blond or Mahogany finish **$329.95** *plus installation* **See your Servel dealer now!**

International Harvester used a new trick to sell the air-conditioning window units above and below. Their model could be covered with fabric by the buyer to blend in with the room colors. They were called the "decorator air conditioners."

Frigidaire built the first room coolers in the late 1920s at a price tag of about $800 each. The company lost a reported $2 million because nobody would buy them. The Servel model above was priced much lower at $329.95.

THE WEATHER
City and State—Fair, Snow, Colder
details in Extra Sections

VOLUME 37 — No. 181

The Metro Daily News

FINAL EDITION

36 PAGES   FIVE CENTS

JUNE 8, 1953

TORNADO STRIKES FLINT, MICH., AREA AND CAUSES 116 DEATHS IN THE BEECHER DISTRICT

The tornado wrecked 340 homes and injured 844 people.

Our Homes

Staying cool in the summer

There was a nationwide heat wave in the United States in 1952 that caused Americans to long for the comfort of air conditioning in their homes. People were growing accustomed to cool stores, offices and restaurants. About 400,000 air conditioners were sold in 1952, compared to 237,000 in 1951. In 1953, about 40 percent of new homes were constructed with air conditioning, though many families continued to rely on fans to keep cool. Air conditioning was still considered a luxury.

General Electric's all-purpose fan had a smart new finger-guard grill and sold for $34.95.

The General Electric automatic twin-fan ventilator above sold for $74.95 and was portable. The floor circulator below was priced at $64.95 and could double as a hassock, table or TV seat.

Hey, it's cool inside! A sunbather is invited to enjoy the comfort of the air-conditioned indoors.

Everyday Life

Hold tight to the everyday moments of life that can slip by so quickly. Those days of raising children could be hectic and exhausting, but were also filled with details that brought smiles to faces years later. Take time to pause and enjoy the cherished moments of hugs, new babies and childhood antics. These lighthearted moments are the best that life offers. Remember those days when you reluctantly washed dishes with a sibling and ended up having fun with a soap-bubble fight? Or when that baby came and seemed to take your place, but you later became the proudest brother or sister ever? The joy of being new parents was incomparable and one of the best parts of everyday life.

"Aw, Mom, do we have to wash the dishes and wear these girly aprons?" Hopefully, these boys grew up to be model husbands who help their wives with meal cleanup.

"That's strange—he's not upstairs, either!"

Dad's home from work, and the children run to be first to sit on his lap. The dog behind the chair may be unhappy that he was dethroned. Or is he patiently waiting for his turn?

A brand-new daughter attracts throngs of visitors. The lonely older brother in the background wonders if everyone has forgotten about him, but there will be plenty of love for all. The math formula for family devotion is: love equals mother plus father times an unlimited number of children.

Grandma is introduced to a grandchild for the first time and can hardly wait to hold the newcomer. The father couldn't be any prouder. And the nurse? These moments are her favorite part of the job.

FAMOUS BIRTHDAYS

Leon Spinks, July 11 boxer (1976 Olympic gold medalist)
Tim Gunn, July 29 TV personality (*Project Runway*)

How hard Mom worked planning the perfect birthday party. She just didn't anticipate the size of childish appetites. Oh no, there's no more ice cream!

Mom stepped outside for just a few moments to bring in the laundry, but time slipped by while chatting with the neighbor. She's about to be surprised by the creative impulses of her little helpers. The child in the chef's hat likely explained, "But Mom, when Dad puts on the chef's hat, the kitchen looks worse than this!"

The Metro Daily News
FINAL EDITION

JULY 25, 1953

"I'M WALKING BEHIND YOU" SUNG BY EDDIE FISHER CLIMBS TO NO. 1 ON THE SONG CHARTS

What started out as a minor paint job mushroomed into a gigantic remodeling project that made everyday life quite interesting and downright crowded for a time.

Everyday Life

Filled with surprises

It was those unexpected moments when our day took a surprising turn that added zest to living. Sometimes the experiences brought pain, but most others swept joy and laughter into our lives we didn't know were missing. That massive kitchen mess the kids created, the birthday party that took a sudden turn, and Junior's experiment with flight will be fondly remembered forever. A strong sense of humor often saved the day.

Being a husband can be a tough life. He can't believe the ladies are still playing bridge when his wife promised the party would be over by the time he came home from work. Besides, shouldn't all these women be home fixing dinner for their families?

"Don't jump!" Mother pleads. Carefree Dad instructs his son to land on the mattress. Siblings and a grandparent cheer on Junior's efforts to fly. Even the neighbors join the assembled audience.

"I made the school band!"

"Yee-haw! Ride 'em cowboy!" This boy could be whoever his imagination dictated as he rode the merry-go-round.

Everyday Life

Just being a kid

Childhood adventures are limited only by the scope of an imagination. It took so little to entertain the children of 1953. Give little girls a large box, clothespins and old curtains, and they were soon enthralled by a grand tea party with dolls as honored guests. The horse on the merry-go-round was magically transformed into the trusty steed of a Western hero. That first night spent in a tent outdoors seemed so exciting during the planning, but after a few ghost stories, bravery was forgotten. What was your most magical childhood moment?

"The drain just said, 'Don't you dare turn on that faucet!'"

The water served for a pretend tea party magically turned into the finest beverage, and the graham crackers were fancy little cakes with a little creative thinking thrown in the mix.

53 SEPS

One of childhood's most fondly remembered adventures is sleeping outside where it is dark and exciting, until some unexplained sound sends the participants running to Mom and Dad and the safety of the house.

1953 HARDWARE MUTUALS

"How 'm I doin', Dad?" What a thrill it is to do a grown-up job, even if it's just for the dog's benefit.

1953 SENTINEL RADIO CORP.

REPRINTED WITH PERMISSION FROM BURLINGTON NORTHERN SANTA FE RAILWAY CO.

Birthday parties shared with friends are well-remembered special occasions.

This boy, decked out in a spacesuit, requests a ticket on the first spaceship to Mars.

THE WEATHER
City and State—Fair,
fresh. Colder
Clouds in Daily Weather

The Metro Daily News

VOLUME 97 — No. 181

FINAL EDITION

20 PAGES   FIVE CENTS

AUGUST 30, 1953

KUKLA, FRAN AND OLLIE SHOW BROADCASTS IN COLOR ON NBC

This children's puppet show starring actress Fran Allison became a favorite for many years.

The crowning touch of school days was that moment when we were handed a diploma. It was a time for goodbyes, yet was bright with hopes for the future.

FAMOUS BIRTHDAYS

Hulk Hogan, August 11 wrestler, actor

Kathie Lee Gifford, August 16 talk-show host (*Regis and Kathie Lee*)

Just the sight of a yellow school bus can bring back memories. Some did homework as the bus lurched and bounced its way along the route while others played cards, told jokes or had heart-to-heart conversations.

Everyday Life

School memories

Gone are the days, but not the memories! What was the best part of those bygone school days? The answers will differ from person to person, but as behavioral scientist B.F. Skinner said, "Education is what survives when what has been learned has been forgotten." Yes, we went to school to learn to read, write and do arithmetic, but the influence of our classmates and teachers also shaped us. Remember the dear, patient home economics teacher? She knew that experience was a better teacher than cookbooks. The thought of going to the principal's office made us quiver with fear, but we learned the meaning of discipline. Ah, those wonderful Golden Rule days.

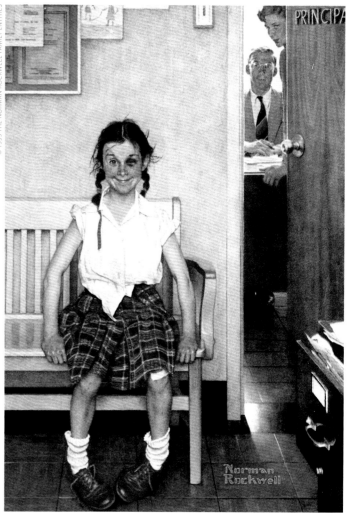

It was most interesting to watch others go through the annual school medical checkup, but not so much fun when you were the one next in line. These "disease detectives" follow up on a diphtheria scare by searching for germ carriers.

This girl is in serious trouble, but you wouldn't know it by the look on her face. She is quite proud of the shiner she received while flattening the school bully.

"Well, don't just stand there; start supporting yourself!"

A luxury that actually does you good

You should use it You'll like to use it...

Prep Time

Women weren't the only ones who spent time in front of the bathroom mirror. A man did his share of sprucing up for the job or his best girl. Shaving was the most monumental yet monotonous task of the daily grooming routine and required both finesse and skill. Most men of the day shaved with a sharp razor aided by a mug, brush and shaving soap. Some used brushless shaving cream such as Burma-Shave, which was also famous for rhyming advertising poems posted on signs along highways. One set of Burma-Shave signs from the 1950s read: He's the guy / The girls forgot / Tho' he was smooth / His face was not!

A splash of Aqua Velva provided the perfect final touch to a shaving routine. Users enjoyed the tingling sensation and pleasant aroma.

The Old Spice brand has years of experience helping guys to smell good with shaving cream, after-shave lotion and soap.

Well-groomed men took pride in smooth, shaved jaws. But watch out for those nicks from sharp blades!

Men were pleased when Schick marketed the injector razor and blades that made the morning routine smoother and more efficient.

Keep hair naturally well-groomed

Vaseline HAIR TONIC

TRADE MARK®

VASELINE is the registered trade mark of the Chesebrough Mfg. Co., Cons'd

Vaseline Hair Tonic helped men achieve the wet look that was so popular in 1953 and also impress a special gal in the process.

The Finest Gift for any man is

365 DAYS OF HAPPY SHAVING

EVERY YEAR !

DE LUXE GIFT PACK
Complete Razor Kit with *Gold Electroplated* Razor and 12 extra-sharp, extra-thick blades *plus* two additional injectors with 24 blades. **ONLY $198**

RAZOR AND LIGHTER GIFT PACK
Complete Kit with *Gold Electro-plated* Razor and 12 blades plus chrome finished Regens Lighter — in handsome gift box. **ONLY $198**

COMPLETE RAZOR KIT
Perfect for home and travel. Bright, handy Travel Kit with *Gold Electroplated* Razor and 12 scalpel-sharp blades. **ONLY 98¢**

YEAR'S SUPPLY OF BLADES
Colorful Holiday Gift Special Package contains 6 Injectors — 120 scalpel-sharp blades. **$439**

Schick Injector Razor and Blades Give
The World's Smoothest, Fastest, Safest Shaves!

Only Schick Injector gives all these advantages: Scalpel-sharp blades change automatically—"lock" at same precise angle—no twisting, no adjusting! Razor "fits" face—under nose, around lips. Safety-Bar smooths down skin—tees up whiskers. So, for happy shaving morning-after-morning—add any Schick Injector Gift Package to *his* Christmas stocking!

Push-Pull, Click-Click!
Blades Locked-Shaves Slick!

give **EVERSHARP SCHICK INJECTOR** *RAZOR & BLADES*

©1953, Eversharp Inc., 350 Fifth Ave., N. Y. C.

Choosing just the right shirt for the occasion required a bit of thought.

THE WEATHER

The Metro Daily News

FINAL EDITION

SEPTEMBER 13, 1953

NIKITA KHRUSHCHEV IS NAMED FIRST SECRETARY OF THE SOVIET COMMUNIST PARTY

Success in a walk!

Hosiery and elegant shoes added that necessary final touch. Nylon hosiery was first made available to women in 1940 and became a huge success. Classic nylons replaced silk stockings and covered about two-thirds of a woman's leg, kept secure by garter belts or girdles. One-piece panty hose were not sold until the 1960s.

FAMOUS BIRTHDAYS

Amy Irving, September 10
actress

Jerry Pate, September 16 PGA
golfer

The time of day and the occasion governed a woman's choice of fragrance, such as Friendship's Garden or Desert Flower, which was carefully applied with an atomizer or a cotton ball.

DESERT FLOWER

REPRINTED WITH PERMISSION FROM THE PROCTOR & GAMBLE CO.

Beautiful Hair

B R E C K

THERE ARE THREE BRECK SHAMPOOS FOR THREE DIFFERENT HAIR CONDITIONS Beautiful hair has natural softness and lustre. A Breck Shampoo will help bring out the soft, natural beauty of your hair. There are three Breck Shampoos. One Breck Shampoo is for dry hair. Another Breck Shampoo is for oily hair. A third Breck Shampoo is for normal hair. The next time you buy a shampoo, select the Breck Shampoo for your individual hair condition. A Breck Shampoo is not drying to the hair, yet it cleans thoroughly. A Breck Shampoo leaves your hair soft, lustrous and naturally beautiful.
The Three Breck Shampoos are available at Beauty Shops, Drug Stores, Department Stores and wherever cosmetics are sold.

JOHN H BRECK INC • MANUFACTURING CHEMISTS • SPRINGFIELD 1 MASSACHUSETTS
NEW YORK • CHICAGO • SAN FRANCISCO • OTTAWA CANADA

Dr. John Breck developed one of the first liquid shampoos in the United States in 1908 and founded the company that produced Breck shampoo. Beginning in 1936, an illustrator by the name of Charles Sheldon created idealized pastel portraits of women with beautiful hair, part of one of America's longest-running ad campaigns.

Prep Time

Achieving the look

To look her best, the woman of 1953 was encouraged by beauty consultants to thoroughly cleanse her face at least twice a day and to always scrub off old makeup before retiring for the night. She should use a suitable foundation base before fluffing powder on her face and carefully apply all makeup so she didn't look "made up." She should give herself a meticulous manicure each week and apply hand lotion daily. And don't forget the undergarments. Girdles were a must to control body lines, and clothes needed to be pressed, in good repair and always appropriate for the occasion. Now she was ready to be seen in public and attract that special man!

A well-groomed woman used both a comb and hairbrush. She was directed to hang her head forward, and using a good bristle brush, move from the scalp to the hair ends.

The girl in a Gossard figures right

Dress by Jacques Fath for Joseph Halpert

Women thought of girdles in terms of flexibility, firmness and smoothness. As for bras, women were advised to select one that gave a firm contour without being injurious!

Figures talk. Maybe yours is criticizing you and your clothes. Which isn't what you want, goodness knows. Neither did this girl. So she changed and we'll tell you how*— how you, too, can have a smarter figure now.

*change to:
Gossard Secret Panel for better tummy control than bones give. Leno and satin elastic in mid-top, hi-top and waistline styles. 14" and 16" lengths. White. **$10** to **$16.50**

*change to:
Flair plunge bra for a shapelier lift from Gossard's satin elastic design. White, pink, black. AA cup, **$3.50**. A, B and C cups, **$3.95**

at leading stores and shops or write us, we'll tell you where

Gossard

THE H. W. GOSSARD CO. • 111 NORTH CANAL STREET • CHICAGO 6
NEW YORK • SAN FRANCISCO • ATLANTA • DALLAS • TORONTO

© 1953 SEPS

Love Is in the Air

Dating in 1953 was a less-rushed affair. People were not as busy, and there was more chance for spontaneous meetings of possible partners. Yes, parents could be annoying at times, but they often guided us toward Mr. or Mrs. Right. Physical appearance was important, but the standards were not quite as superficial. A popular dating guide from the 1950s stated that many practical considerations may have been ignored in teenage culture because there was so much emphasis on romance. Marriage was addressed, too. "Studies of marriage show that a determination to succeed is a big factor in the success of a marriage." That piece of advice continues to be true.

Their daughter has just returned home after a date with the most wonderful, handsome boy in the whole world and is dreamily sharing the details with her mother. What about Father? He pretends to be asleep but is making sure he knows the scoop too.

To be glamorous is this gal's goal, so she even takes a beauty kit to the beach. Her date seems to appreciate her efforts to look good.

1953 VIRGINIA-CAROLINA CHEMICAL CORP.

This couple is studying more than just the book. They are assessing each other as future marriage material as well.

© 1953 SEPS

Mothers are wonderful people, but why must they share the baby pictures with every girl brought home? No, not the bathing photo too!

Who is happier here, the couple choosing the engagement ring or the jeweler who is making a fine sale?

At last, the day and the hour have arrived, and the couple is joined in marriage. They are composed, but every woman in the room is teary-eyed with joy.

"Smaller pieces, dear."

The handsome couple poses for an official outdoor wedding portrait.

The bride wore a dress of ivory silk with a bouffant skirt embellished with more than 50 yards of flounces. Her veil, first worn by Jacqueline's Grandmother Lee, was draped from a tiara. The bridal bouquet consisted of pink and white orchids and gardenias.

The beaming bride and groom cut the ornate wedding cake ordered by Joseph Kennedy.

The bride is escorted by her groom and Charles Bartlett down a hill at their wedding reception. Others looking on are Edward Kennedy and Torbert MacDonald. An estimated 3,000 people tried to gate-crash the reception to catch a glimpse of the famous couple and guests.

John F. Kennedy Weds Jacqueline Bouvier

John F. Kennedy, the ambitious Massachusetts politician, met high-society beauty Jacqueline Bouvier in 1951 and was impressed by her loveliness and intelligence. They shared many interests, so it was just a matter of time before the senator proposed. The wedding took place in a picturesque Roman Catholic church in Newport, R.I., on Sept. 12, 1953, and was considered by many to be the social event of the year. More than 800 guests, including many famous people, witnessed the celebration that rivaled anything in Hollywood for star appeal and glamour.

The Kennedy siblings at the wedding reception are, clockwise from left: Robert F. Kennedy, Patricia Kennedy, Eunice Kennedy Shriver, Edward M. Kennedy, Jean Kennedy, John F. Kennedy and Jacqueline Bouvier Kennedy.

Senator John F. Kennedy and Jacqueline Bouvier Kennedy dance under a huge canopy to the music of Meyer Davis and his orchestra. The wedding reception was held at Hammersmith Farm, an oceanfront estate in Newport, R.I.

This soda-fountain clerk must have a special aura about him, with three girls and even the dog making eyes at him.

"Hi! I see you got my note."

Around the Neighborhood

During the 1950s, neighborhood stores were plentiful and usually within walking distance for town residents. Most of the stores were small specialty shops. The bakery was stocked with everything from basic dinner rolls, and hot dog and hamburger buns to cinnamon rolls and doughnuts. The scent that drifted out the door was nearly irresistible. The freshest of produce and prime cuts of meat were carefully displayed at the grocery. The fire department, with its red fire truck, was a fixture in most towns, and the post office and soda fountain were hubs of activity.

As this small boy dreams of someday driving the shiny red fire truck and ringing the bell, the grown-ups relive their own memories of that first ride.

The postmaster's day is livened by a visit from these three brave little keepers of the law, hot on the trail of a wanted desperado.

To the dismay of his mother and the consternation of the grocer, a boy disturbs the carefully constructed pile of oranges.

The park, sometimes called the village green, was a spot for relaxing. Each person had his or her own way of unwinding. Youngsters got their exercise, while others preferred to sit on the benches and observe.

Luscious cakes tempt the baker to abandon his diet in favor of tastier fare.

Convair speeds you on your way
...*after the flight, too!*

If you're the kind of air traveler who likes *convenience* with speed and luxury...then welcome aboard the Convair.

From nimble takeoff to sure-footed landing, the Convair is a model of engineering efficiency. And its exclusive hand-baggage racks and self-contained stairway speed you on your way *after* the flight, too! No more baggage claiming lines. Often you'll save 30 minutes or more on arrival.

Ask your favorite airline or travel agent to make your next flight a Convair...the world's most popular passenger plane, with built-in *get-up-and-go!*

As a transport-trainer for the U.S. Air Force, the Convair is setting new records for versatility and performance...another evidence of Convair's Engineering to the Nth Power

CONVAIR
SAN DIEGO AND POMONA, CALIFORNIA
FORT WORTH AND DAINGERFIELD, TEXAS

MORE AIRLINES HAVE CHOSEN THE CONVAIR THAN ANY OTHER MODERN PASSENGER PLANE: NOW FLYING: Aerolineas Argentinas • Aero O/Y, Finland • Alitalia, Italy • American • Braniff • Canadian Pacific • Continental • Delta-C&S • Ethiopian • Hawaiian • KLM Royal Dutch • Linee Aeree Italiane, Italy • National • Northeast • Orient, Pakistan • PAL, Philippine • Pan American • Republic of Indonesia • Sabena, Belgium • Swissair, Switzerland • Trans Australia • United • Western — **SOON TO FLY:** Aeronaves De Mexico • Avensa, Venezuela • CMA, Mexico • Cruzeiro do Sul, Brazil • JAT, Jugoslavia • Lufthansa, Germany • Real S. A., Brazil

The airlines boasted delicious meals, friendly service, and above all, speedy travel.

Traveling on the California Zephyr train was a memorable experience. In one of the Vista-Domes, the view was amazing. The train also had a buffet lounge car and dining car.

A Pullman sleeping car had plenty of room for the family and a big, comfortable bed in which to stretch out.

Travel Adventures

When it came to travel in 1953, the options for reaching your destination were varied. Thanks to the airlines, we could travel to glamorous destinations such as Paris, Hawaii or Rome. In some cases, domestic travel by plane was cost comparable to a railroad ticket. United Air Lines offered flights from Chicago to New York for about $45, compared to the cost of a first-class trip by rail priced at $49.95. Most people still chose to travel by train or bus, where they could take their time and enjoy the scenery.

The smart man or woman gave the family car a rest and chose to travel by Greyhound bus. A three-day tour of the Great Smoky Mountains included eight meals and cost $50 per person. A trip through the Grand Canyon and Utah Parks lasted five days and included 15 meals, all for $78.

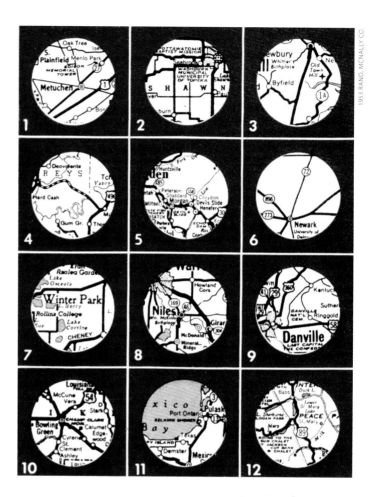

1953 RAND, McNALLY CO.

There's **One Sure Way**

to have a glorious carefree vacation

SE GREYHOUND'S

Vacation **P**lanning **S**ervice

Where Do You Think You Are?

East or west, north or south, each of the distinctive areas above appeared on the road map of a single state in 1953. There is, as the saying goes, "no place like it." Can you identify the states?

Answers: 1-New Jersey; 2-Kansas; 3-Massachusetts; 4-Mississippi; 5-Utah; 6-Delaware; 7-Florida; 8-Ohio; 9-Virginia; 10-Missouri; 11-New York; 12-Montana

Travel Adventures
The fun of getting away

All those hours spent driving to see the view at Point Lookout, and the children would rather read books. Dad just doesn't understand why they don't appreciate his efforts. All this natural beauty should be enjoyed.

What better place is there to spend a hot summer day than at camp? The creek water is cool and refreshing, and no one cares if watermelon juice runs down your chin. Don't forget the watermelon-seed–spitting contest! Later there will be canoeing and maybe even a night spent in a real teepee.

"Everything's just as I imagined it would be—soft breezes, tropical moon, romantic music and no men!"

The Metro Daily News

FINAL EDITION

OCTOBER 10, 1953

WINKY DINK AND YOU DEBUTS ON CBS NETWORK

This interactive TV show for children was shown on Saturday mornings and hosted by Jack Barry.

Fathers everywhere tend to have the urge to drive nonstop with only the destination in mind. Luckily for this family, they managed to get the last room in the motor court.

Why is it when a couple finally manages to find a quiet hideaway, they don't remain alone for long? Out of all the sand dunes, this mob, complete with picnic basket and dog, just had to choose this particular area.

The men are roughing it for the weekend, but are finding that a woman's work is never done. Maybe after the laundry, mending and cooking are finished, they will find time to fish.

Winner's Circle

It's been said, "You play to win the game." The individuals and teams featured here did just that. They were all winners, not just because they were talented, but as a result of motivation, determination and old-fashioned hard work. For example, hockey player Gordie Howe immersed himself in the sport, playing every day of the year and using not only a hockey puck to practice, but also tennis balls or even clumps of dirt. This type of dedication, exhibited by all the champions of 1953, was a shining example of the way to success. One winning team not shown here was the Montreal Canadiens, who won the Stanley Cup over the Boston Bruins 4 games to 1.

The Detroit Lions triumphed 17-16 over the Cleveland Browns in the 1953 NFL Championship Game. Head coach Raymond "Buddy" Parker was lifted on the shoulders of his players after the win. The game was televised on the DuMont network and the attendance at the stadium was 54,577.

Pouring it on lap after lap, Indianapolis 500 winner Bill Vukovich averaged 128.74 mph to win America's toughest auto race in searing heat.

FAMOUS BIRTHDAYS
Tony Shalhoub, October 9 actor (Adrian of *Monk*)
Keith Hernandez, October 20 baseball player (St. Louis Cardinals, New York Mets)

The Minneapolis Lakers trounced the New York Knicks 4 games to 1 to win the NBA Championship. The score of the final game was 91-84. This title was the Lakers' fourth of five wins in the period from 1949 to 1954.

Gordie Howe of the Detroit Red Wings was chosen as the 1953 NHL MVP and leading scorer. He is considered one of the most durable players of all time, playing 26 seasons over five decades.

Neva Langley from Georgia was crowned as the 1953 Miss America. Her talent was a piano performance, and after time off to be a mother and an active volunteer to organizations, she was a featured piano soloist with symphony orchestras.

Winner's Circle
The champs

In 1953, tennis star Maureen Connolly became the first woman to win the "Grand Slam" as she was the women's singles champion at Wimbledon, the French Open, the U.S. Open and the Australian Open. Her achievements propelled her into the spotlight, and she became the darling of the media and one of the most popular people in the United States at the time.

Vic Seixas was one of the top tennis players during the 1950s. In 1953 he won the men's singles championship at Wimbledon; he is shown here with his trophy.

American Carl "Bobo" Olson, right, won the World Middleweight Championship over Great Britain's Randolph Turpin at Madison Square Garden in New York City. Olson was a tough fighter with skill, determination, grit and a love of boxing.

Golfer Ben Hogan tees off during the 1953 Masters Tournament at Augusta, Ga. Hogan's well-deserved win was the result of his work ethic and his ability to perform well under pressure. He had his greatest year in 1953, triumphing with his second Masters, his fourth U.S. Open and his only British Open.

© GETTY IMAGES

ETTY IMAGES

Racehorse owner A.G. Vanderbilt is shown with his horse Native Dancer and jockey Eric Guerin after winning the Belmont Stakes. Native Dancer was named the Champion 3-Year-Old Colt of 1953.

Winner's Circle

Take me out to the ball game

In 1953, baseball retained its hold on the title of the "national pastime" because it was the most widely played sport in the country. Women had their own network of teams called the All-American Girls Professional Baseball League, formed during World War II to continue the baseball tradition while many men went to war. In men's baseball, "The Bronx Bombers," or the Yankees, and "The Bums from Brooklyn," as the Dodgers were called, returned for yet another "Subway Series," as the duel of New York's great teams was called. The Yankee dynasty continued with a record fifth consecutive World Series championship. The Yankees won in six games, and the score of the final game was 4-3.

In 1953, the Grand Rapids Chicks won the All-American Girls Professional Baseball League Championship.

Jean Faut of the South Bend Blue Sox, was the All-American Girls Professional Baseball League Player of the Year for 1953. She was a right-handed pitcher and infielder who gave the league and its fans nine excellent seasons. She was admired for her competitive nature on the field.

NATIONAL BASEBALL HALL OF FAME LIBRARY COOPERSTOWN, N.Y.

New York Yankees players congratulate each other on their successful season. They are, from left to right, Hank Bauer, Yogi Berra, Billy Martin and Joe Collins.

The Metro Daily News

FINAL EDITION

NOVEMBER 17, 1953

ST. LOUIS BROWNS OFFICIALLY BECOME THE BALTIMORE ORIOLES

OFFICIAL PROGRAM • FIFTY CENTS

NEW YORK

Yankees

GOLDEN ANNIVERSARY WORLD SERIES

1903   1953

BROOKLYN **Dodgers**

The Yankees players welcome Mickey Mantle back to the dugout after his grand slam during the 1953 World Series played against the Brooklyn Dodgers.

Billy Martin is tagged by Roy Campanella for the final out of game four of the 1953 World Series.

Carl Furillo of the Brooklyn Dodgers scores a run, beating the throw to New York Yankees catcher Yogi Berra.

Gardening became a new No. 1 leisure occupation. After being a necessity for many years, it was now possible to grow plants just for the pleasure of their beauty.

The artist has stepped back to assess her masterpiece, but the puzzled farmer is not sure what she's seeing. Maybe if he tilts his head in the other direction, he'll catch on to the joys of modern art.

One of the most satisfying aspects of stamp collecting is the friendly contact with other enthusiasts, as these boys discovered.

All work and no play makes Jack a dull boy. A little fishing on the side breathes new life into a fellow.

Leisure Activities

In 1953, most Americans enjoyed an increase in leisure time. The average employee worked 40 hours a week and was given several weeks of vacation each year. With all of this extra free time, Americans were finding new ways to unwind and indulge. According to *Fortune* magazine, in 1953 Americans spent more than $30 billion on leisure activities and goods. Millions of people participated in sports like boating, golf, bowling and fishing. Many more fans attended football, baseball and basketball games, while others watched the sports on TV.

This is a shooting gallery, using real bullets, yet the couple is oblivious to the looks of disapproval around them. What is she aiming at? Likely it's matrimony!

The weather has warmed and the golf course beckons. This wife is one step ahead of her husband, with a message written on the car that desperately needs a wash and wax.

"Now doesn't this beat staying out all night with the boys?"

Leisure Activities

Written words

With the expansion of leisure time in America, people became enthusiastic readers. Books about religion, cooking, homemaking and do-it-yourself projects were among the top sellers. People also read romance and mystery novels by the dozens. Bookstores experienced an increase in sales due partly to the popularity of comic books and paperbacks. In 1953, there was a trend toward adapting books to the big screen. *The Robe, The Silver Chalice, Désirée, Battle Cry* and *From Here to Eternity* were all books on the best-seller list that became movies.

Comic books were popular in 1953, with their colorful illustrations and exciting story lines.

Breakfast With a Bang

By Norman R. Jaffray

Up pops the cereal,
More energized than most,
And up pops the toast machine
And out pops the toast.

Up pops the coffeepot
Above a head of steam,
And up pops the bottle top
To liberate the cream.

Up pops the minute hand
Of the electric clock,
And up pop the husbands all
To scurry down the block.

Missing Ingredient

By James E. Power

My wallet's stuffed with cards that state
My right to vote, to hunt, to drive,
To borrow books, to have a mate,
To hold a job, to be alive;
With stubs and checks to help me claim
My laundry, cleaning, coat and hat;
With forms that show my age, my name,
My height, my weight, if thin or fat,
The color of my eyes and hair,
Identifying marks or scars,

If I'm ruddy, dark or fair,
My membership in private bars;
With pictures of my kids and wife;
With statements of financial worth;
With records of my Army life;
With proof of date and place of birth;
With licenses, permits and notes;
With bills I've paid and bills I owe;
With clippings, quips and clever quotes …
With everything, in fact, but dough.

POEMS FEATURED ON PAGES 92 AND 93 WERE REPRINTED WITH PERMISSION FROM *THE SATURDAY EVENING POST*.

The book titled *The Robe* was written back in 1942. It became a top-selling novel again when a movie version of the book was released in 1953. Stars Richard Burton and Jean Simmons, center, are pictured in a scene from *The Robe*.

The Girls Get Together

By Celia Keegan

The girls and I have sipped our tea
And bandied gossip brightly
With much discourse of He and She …
And stifled yawns politely.

The TV flickers on, unwatched;
The undealt cards are scattered;
A rumor's fed, a rumor's scotched,
As if it really mattered.

The "boys" will join us soon, they said.
Our gathering's still the hen kind
We'd be no duller, were we dead,
Thus parted from our menkind.

Discussions rise and fall again,
All interest pseudo-hearty.
Ah, now's the time for all good men
To come to the aid of the party!

Song for a New Year

By Marian P. Fickes

The whistles blow
And look what's here:
A brand-new leaf,
A brand-new year,

A brand-new twig
On Time's old tree,
A brand-new dress …
On the same old me!

Best-Selling Books of 1953

The Robe
by Lloyd C. Douglas

The Silver Chalice
by Thomas B. Costain

Désirée
by Annemarie Selinko

Battle Cry
by Leon M. Uris

From Here to Eternity
by James Jones

The High and the Mighty
by Ernest K. Gann

Beyond This Place
by A.J. Cronin

Time and Time Again
by James Hilton

Lord Vanity
by Samuel Shellabarger

The Unconquered
by Ben Ames Williams

What Made Us Laugh

"Any children?"

"All right … your turn."

"It was a daring gown till Mother got her hands on it."

"Dear me, I've been waiting so long I think I've recovered."

"Read that last paragraph again—
it doesn't seem to make any sense."

"Fine spacious basement, snug and dry …"

"Do you have anything a little more ridiculous?"

Country folks had a ready supply of fresh food at hand. Dairy operations produced milk and tasty milk byproducts such as butter and cheese. Many families planted a few fruit trees on their land to bring in extra income and fill canning jars and freezers for homegrown flavor all year through.

Teacher rings a bell to call all students to the classroom, but the future football stars are so absorbed in their pickup game in the large school yard that they tune out the summons.

Follow the leader, wherever he may go. The boy with the oars is in control of this party with his friends unable to see the way from underneath the boat. But wait—he's going the wrong way if he's planning to boat on the lake.

Living in the Country

The fresh breezes and open spaces of the country held a variety of memories for those who chose to put down roots in rural communities. "The cows are out!" was a sentence that could strike fear into the heart of the hardiest farmer. The family was quickly rounded up to chase the bovines back to their enclosure before a disastrous encounter with a car or the neighbor's cornfield could be chewed to bits. Country children had nearly limitless places to play. Opportunities for adventure were abundant with fields, barns, creeks and ponds to explore.

Spring has arrived, and the scent of apple blossoms perfumes the air, accompanied by the fun of jumping rope and going barefoot. Isn't the boy a little gentleman to help the girls skip rope? Don't worry, it won't be long until he lassoes them with it and ties them to the tree, cowboy style.

Having made their way out of the tangle of city traffic, these folks were enjoying the serenity of wide-open spaces until a herd of cows on the loose formed a new sort of traffic jam.

FAMOUS BIRTHDAYS
Dennis Miller, November 3 comic, talk-show host, author (*Saturday Night Live*)
Harry Carson, November 26 NFL linebacker (New York Giants)

City Living

The city was an exciting, colorful and energetic place to live in 1953. The stores were large and had wide selections to make shopping a real treat. A whole day could speed by while window-shopping or cruising the aisles of department stores. Though there were fewer green spaces than in the country for those inclined to be outdoors, parks provided trees, grass and places to meet and greet fellow city dwellers. The variety of entertainment was diverse. People could choose from unusual cuisines that originated in distant countries and enjoy music or plays any day of the week.

Central Park in New York City is a green oasis in the midst of the tall buildings. People can hike, bike, boat, ride a horse or get lost in a small woods.

Feeding peanuts to the elephants is the highlight of a trip to the zoo, until the gigantic beasts decide to spray a little water for fun.

"What's he waiting for?"

At the world-famous Tiffany's jewelry store in New York City, a vast assortment of gems are displayed at their sparkling best.

There are many places to visit in the city where people can dress in their best and enjoy the finest of music.

SILVER SLIPPER GRILL

norman rockwell

An abundance of churches are within walking distance in the city for the family who makes regular worship a priority.

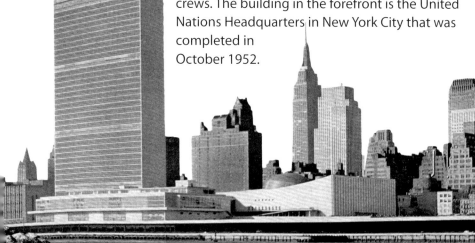

A city skyline is a majestic scene attesting to the talents of both architects and construction crews. The building in the forefront is the United Nations Headquarters in New York City that was completed in October 1952.

"If my husband were here he could figure this out in a jiffy—in fact we could stick him with the whole thing!"

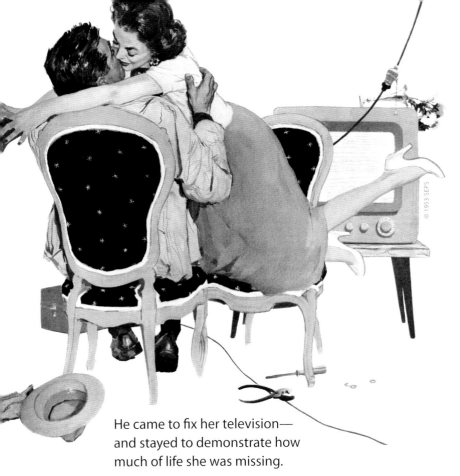

He came to fix her television—
and stayed to demonstrate how
much of life she was missing.

It was dangerous, having secret dates with her
ex-husband. It was so easy to forget she wasn't
married to him anymore.

She belonged on a
rich man's yacht; he
was a common sailor.
How could he think
of marriage? She was
obviously out of his class.

Leading Ladies of *The Post*

Take a peek at some of the art inside the covers of *The Saturday Evening Post*. The Leading Ladies of *The Post* are a collection of images from regularly featured steamy romance stories. Illustrators were challenged to interpret these stories on canvas, and we have included a sampling of the Leading Ladies of 1953. The sultry fashion-forward heroines of the tales are featured along with the original article captions.

He put up with a lot from his wife—because he loved her. But he couldn't stand it forever, being married to the woman who liked to flirt.

He couldn't understand why she got angry when he proposed. He knew he was a catch for any woman.

Did he recognize, in this sleek, glamorous girl from the city, the fat, freckle-faced kid she had been? Would he be sorry, now, that he had scorned the ugly duckling?

1953 Fashion

Elegant style

A high-fashion designer from France by the name of Christian Dior set the clothing trends of the 1950s. American women wanted to wear something new and refreshing, and Dior's designs fit the bill. "I wanted my dresses to be constructed, molded upon the curves of the feminine body, whose sweep they would stylize," said the renowned designer. Dior made about $7 million a year with his fashions. A simple day dress cost about $300, while a lacy, embroidered ball gown could set Dior enthusiasts back about $2,400.

At a 1953 showing of his creations, Christian Dior said he created "to please the ladies by enabling them to please their men."

Nearly half of Dior's revenues came from the United States. The designer also authorized replicas of his creations that sold for much less than the original designs.

The 48-year-old Dior, fashion designer extraordinaire, would revise gowns up until the minute they were shown.

MEMORABLE QUOTE

"Aren't people crazy to spend so much on a dress!"

—Christian Dior

There are few luxuries that can delight a lady quite like a sable coat. Standing in the photo above is designer and salesman Michael Maximilian along with models wearing a $43,500 crown sable cape and $10,000 stole.

Actress Patricia Neal looks over a jewel assortment in a private showroom located at Tiffany's in New York City. The high-fashion look of 1953 was well-bred, perfectly manicured, and ladylike—and the right accessories were the key to pulling it all off.

Jeweled accessories from Tiffany's are some of the little things that can make a woman look like a million bucks. The diamond brooch, top right, divided into a pair of clips and cost $13,800. The diamond bracelet in the center sold for $20,400, and the diamond brooch in the lower left was $7,850.

"How's that again? All I heard was mumbledollars and 98 cents."

Fashioned with finesse, colorful and washable dresses sold for $4 to $5 each.

Misses new-season tweeds and corduroys sold for $8 to $10. Stunning, high-style fashions like the dress above and the suit at right were made of fine quality fabric with interesting details and could be purchased from a Montgomery Ward catalog.

Pedal pushers or slacks were worn for leisure hours and were priced at about $5.

1953 MONTGOMERY WARD

1953 Fashion

The traditional woman

So you didn't have a large stash of cash to spend on your wardrobe? Never fear, a woman could still be stylish in 1953 even if she couldn't afford designer clothing. Clothing manufacturers mass-produced the latest look so all women could look classy. The top designers began to allow these companies to buy designs to copy. The clothes were disassembled until they could be laid flat and used as basic patterns. American women liked the idea of choosing a dress from a store and being able to wear it the same day without waiting for a designer to work his magic.

© 1953 SEPS

"My husband has very definite tastes. He can't stand me in anything over 20 dollars."

A perfect suit, like the one below by Handmacher, took full advantage of a woman's figure. The tailored look sold for about $60.

1953 MONTGOMERY WARD

Versatile, new sweater styles were made of nylon that wouldn't shrink when washed and were quick-drying. The 1953 price was about $3 each.

1953 MONTGOMERY WARD

1953 HANDMACHER-VOGEL INC.

The coat at left was constructed of camel's hair and wool. The good-quality coat was $39.98, the better-quality was $49.98 and best-quality coat sold for $59.98.

1953 Fashion

Women's classy coats

The perfect coat was the final touch for a fashionable winter outfit and kept out the chill on wintery cold days. Coats came in two basic styles in the 1953 Montgomery Ward catalog. Some were designed to be full and flowing, while others hugged the figure and had belts to emphasize a tiny waist. Most coats were constructed of long-wearing, mothproof wool and cashmere. Some styles were sold in different quality grades at graduated prices in categories labeled good, better and best. The same look was made affordable for all.

The belt of the red wool coat at left made a free-flowing coat take on fitted lines. The blue coat at left was trimmed with mouton fur, a fancy name for sheepskin that was cut and dyed to resemble beaver fur. Combined with 100 percent virgin wool and lined with taffeta, this coat featured gracious shirred sleeves and sold for $39.98.

FAMOUS BIRTHDAYS
Kim Basinger, December 8
actress
Barry Livingston, December 17
actor (Ernie Douglas of *My Three Sons*)

1953 MONTGOMERY WARD

Fine fur trim of fox, Russian marmot or Persian lamb added elegance to the coats of 1953. The bodies of the three coats at left were constructed of American poodle cloth for the new nubby look. Prices ranged from $59.98 to $79.98.

The back details of these casual coats had as many interesting details as the front. Both sold for about $20. The coat at left had velveteen trim and a sparkling buckle. The deep V-yoke of the coat above set off a flowing style with full sleeves and flyaway cuffs.

This selection of the Manhattan clothing line was advertised as the quality way to tell Dad he's still the leader of your band on Father's Day. The dress shirt was $3.95, ties $1.50 to $2.50, sport shirt $5, pajama top $5 and shorts $1.25.

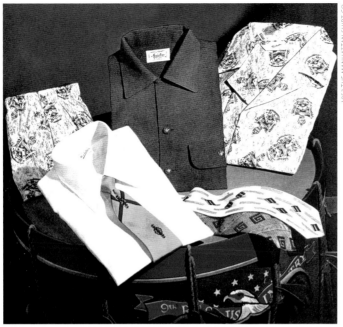

1953 THE MANHATTAN SHIRT CO.

SWANK
makes the difference

1953 SWANK INC

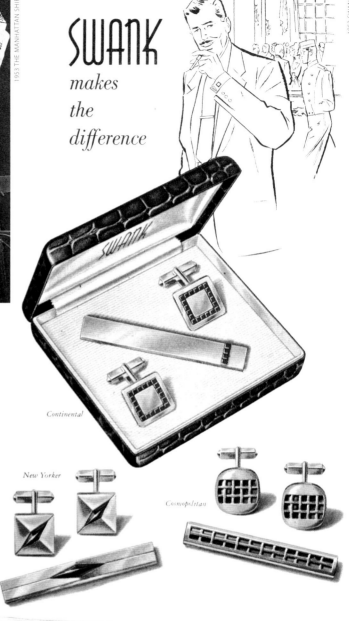

Continental

New Yorker

Cosmopolitan

A special bond is created between a father and son when a youngster begins to care about how he looks. Dad's duty was to teach his son how to properly tie his tie.

1953 HART SCHAFFNER & MARX

The Metro Daily News

THE WEATHER
City and State—Rain. Snow, Colder

VOLUME 47 — No. 361

FINAL EDITION

79 PAGES   FIVE CENTS

DECEMBER 12, 1953

WORLD WAR II FIGHTER PILOT CHUCK YEAGER SHATTERS THE SPEED RECORD
He attains Mach 2.43 in a Bell X-1A rocket plane.

1953 Fashion

The man about town

Fashions for men's clothing in 1953 were based on business attire. If a man had a job at an office, it was expected that he wear a suit, shirt and tie along with cuff links every day. The look was conservative and rather colorless except for the ties which were often boldly colored with interesting patterns. Taking off a suit jacket was not proper unless a man was at home; there, he could relax in his white shirt and suit trousers.

"I'm just looking!"

The addition of nylon mesh to shoes created a new look that was also cool and comfortable to wear in hot weather.

A man was not properly dressed without a hat. A hat's color should match the suit in shades of dark blue, gray, charcoal or brown. This Mallory hat sold for $10.

Suits and coats were sometimes made of rugged, colorful and comfortable tweed. The topcoat had comfortable, deep wing sleeves and a vented back.

1953 Fashion

Dressing the kids

Most families in this post-war era could afford to spend more on clothes. Instead of having just a Sunday suit and a few changes of clothes for wear throughout the week, boys now had several different outfits to choose from. Young girls rarely wore slacks to school. Their mothers dressed them in skirts, blouses or feminine frilly dresses. Full skirts were the standard on most dresses. Girls did wear slacks for playwear at home.

The velveteen set above was fur trimmed and cost $21.98. The set at upper right was easily adjusted for growth. The toddler girls' and boys' outerwear at right cost from $7.98 to $9.98.

The boys' cotton Western shirts sold for $1.98 each. The sturdy plaid cotton broadcloth shirts were $1.79 each. The sizes ranged from 6–18.

The ski pants above were warmly lined with practical knee patches and cost about $5. The corduroy coat and ski pants at left sold for $13.98 in sizes 4–8.

1953 MONTGOMERY WARD

The girls' warm sportswear at left was priced from $1.79 for the flannel shirt to $2.79 for the corduroy slacks. The girls' hard-wearing jeans below had a side zipper and cost $1.98.

Girls' smartly detailed cotton dresses in the top row came in sizes 7–14 and sold for $3.98. The dainty dresses for toddlers in the bottom row were priced from $1.98 to $2.98.

The boys' matching casual set and the two-piece set both cost $4. Toddler girls' overalls cost from $1.98 to $2.49.

The toy service station at left was like the real thing—everything worked. It cost $4.39, was shipped flat and labeled as "easily assembled."

The official Lone Ranger cowgirl and cowboy outfits below were well-made to withstand rough-and-tumble play, and cost $4.79 each.

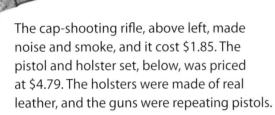

The cap-shooting rifle, above left, made noise and smoke, and it cost $1.85. The pistol and holster set, below, was priced at $4.79. The holsters were made of real leather, and the guns were repeating pistols.

This six-piece Lone Ranger sports kit cost $3.69.

The Lone Ranger records, priced from $3.98 to $4.89, were the recordings from five shows. The portable phonograph sold for $29.95.

Toy Time

Were you the proud owner of any of the toys pictured here? Perhaps you saved every penny you could from your allowance to buy a coveted bike, Western item or View-Master. *The Lone Ranger* was a popular television show about a masked rider of the West in search of justice. The Lone Ranger rode again when a boy or girl wore costumes from the show. View-Master joined forces with Walt Disney Studios to produce reels of color transparencies from the popular Disney movies.

A View-Master was a popular way to look at brilliant Kodachromes that came on paper disks with 14 slides that combined to make seven scenes. The lighting unit, stereoscope hand viewer and projector above were priced separately. The deluxe outfit was $5.98 and included a stereoscope, choice of six disks and a box for storage.

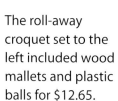

The roll-away croquet set to the left included wood mallets and plastic balls for $12.65.

1953 MONTGOMERY WARD

The juvenile bikes above were made of steel. The deluxe 24-inch bike, far right, had chrome fenders, a built-in electric horn and headlight that operated on batteries. The price was $51.45.

Toy Time
Treasures of childhood

Inlay education puzzles were constructed of brightly colored pressed board. There was an alphabet puzzle, a U.S. map puzzle and one world map puzzle. The cost was $1.49 for the set of three.

This spelling and counting board sold for $.89 and featured sliding wooden blocks with letters on one side and numbers on the other.

These soft vinyl dolls could drink from a bottle, wet, coo and sleep. They had glass eyes with lashes and movable heads, arms and legs, and sold for $1.75 each. Little girls could practice their sewing skills with the kit in the leather box. The kit included everything needed to sew three outfits, including buttons, trim and thread, and sold with one of the dolls for $7.49.

This train for toddlers was ideal for a child's first train on wheels. It was made of wood and could be easily taken apart and put back together. The price was $3.49.

Krazy Ikes was a plastic, durable construction toy for kids. It was easy to make the funny figures. The set included bodies, heads, feet, joints and connections for $1.79.

1953 MONTGOMERY WARD

1953 MONTGOMERY WARD

1953 MONTGOMERY WARD

This Playskool peg-and-nail table and bench with blackboard cost $3.79 and could keep youngsters happy and absorbed for hours. It came with wooden pieces that represented trees and houses for creating scenes and a removable pounding board, wooden sticks and blocks, and metal hammer.

Dolls, dolls and more dolls are shown here. The 14- to 17-inch dolls in the top row ranged from $4.95 to $12.45. The dainty bride doll, top row, included curlers for the hair. The doll in the blue dress was all plastic and guaranteed unbreakable. The hair could be "permanent waved." The miniature dolls in the second row were 7½ inches tall with movable heads and arms, and sleeping eyes, priced at $1.67 each. The miniatures in the bottom row included Walt Disney's Tinker Bell and Peter Pan.

Decorated glass ornaments in brilliant colors brightened the Christmas tree.

What a special moment it was when a loved one opened a gift that was chosen with love and care.

Vintage plastic snowman and Santa figurines added a merry touch to the season's decorations.

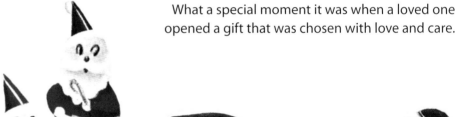

Illuminated, weatherproof Christmas decorations lit the night and beamed holiday cheer to all.

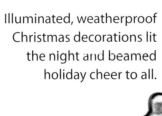

Christmas Traditions

Christmas is more than gift-giving, cheery decor and tasty food. That special Christmas feeling returns yearly as the tree is decorated, lights are strung, and gifts are gathered and wrapped with loving thoughts of those who will open them. The climax arrives when people gather at churches to remember the One who came to earth on a silent, holy night. There is a feeling that no matter how imperfect people are, there is hope for a future of unity, peace and goodness. What an encouraging and merry feeling we celebrate at Christmas.

During a quiet, reflective moment in a Christmas service, the children's choir enters singing familiar carols and carrying lighted candles.

Santa and one of his reindeer delight children in the snow outside his workshop.

"... something on the order of Gregory Peck!"

Instead of digging out solid shortening, you *pour* this light, sparkling salad oil—the one and only Wesson. Because it *pours*, you measure Wesson accurately. No waste. Wesson is *thrifty*. And—in all the world, there's no oil lighter or more delicate than Wesson Oil. So Wesson protects the flavor of your best cakes and pies and cookies—to delight your own folks or for happy holiday giving.

WESSON'S FAMOUS FRUITCAKE

Wesson Oil simplifies the method—brings out luscious fruit-nut flavor. *Heat oven to 275° (slow).*

Mix together ....{
- 1 cup Wesson Oil
- 1½ cups brown sugar (packed in cup)
- 4 eggs

Beat vigorously with spoon or electric mixer for 2 minutes.

Sift together ....{
- 2 cups *sifted* Gold Medal all-purpose flour
- *1 teasp. double-action baking powder
- *2 teasp. salt
- 2 teasp. cinnamon
- 2 teasp. allspice
- 1 teasp. cloves

Stir into oil mixture alternately with...
Mix ....
- 1 cup pineapple, apple or orange juice
- 1 cup more *sifted* flour

into ....{
- 1 cup thinly sliced citron
- 1 cup chopped candied pineapple
- 1½ cups whole candied cherries
- 1 cup raisins
- 1 cup chopped figs
- 1 cup coarsely chopped Diamond® Walnuts
- 2 cups coarsely chopped mixed nuts

Pour batter over fruit, mixing thoroughly.
Line with brown paper 2 greased loaf pans, 8½ x 4½ x 2½-in. Pour batter into pans. Place a pan of water on lower oven rack. Bake cakes 2½ to 3 hours in slow oven (275°). After baking, let cakes stand 15 minutes before removing from pans. Cool thoroughly on racks without removing paper. When cool, remove paper. To insure freshness, seal in cellophane or heavy waxed paper with "Scotch" Cellophane Tape, then put in covered container in a cool place to ripen. For holiday gifts, add a decorative bow of "Sasheen" ribbon.
When using Gold Medal Self-Rising Flour, omit baking powder and salt.

Wesson Oil

Wesson Oil
Your Liquid Shortening

Christmas Traditions

Holiday baking

Say the word "Christmas," and most folks instantly recall the heavenly scents that wafted through the air during the season. Mom spent hours in the kitchen creating sumptuous desserts and sweet treats of all kinds that were so tempting and delicious. This collection of recipes from 1953 ads will bring back the memories of Christmas cakes and candy cane cookies.

Swans Down Cherry-Go-Round Christmas Cake recipe shown on page 119.

Swans Down Cherry-Go-Round Christmas Cake

It's more luscious, more homemade-tasting than any cake you could *ever* make with a mix! It's more melt-in-your-mouth-able than even a cake genius could make with "bread flour."

Swans Down Cake Flour plus your own good ingredients will give you a cake as delicate as this every time. And you'll spend *less* than if you'd used a mix!

2¼ cups sifted Swans Down Cake Flour
3¼ teaspoons Calumet Baking Powder
1 teaspoon salt   1½ cups sugar
½ cup shortening (at room temperature)
1 cup milk   1½ teaspoons vanilla
¼ teaspoon almond extract
4 egg whites, unbeaten
2 tablespoons finely cut maraschino cherries
¾ cup chopped nuts

Mixing. (Mix by hand or at a low speed of electric mixer. Count only actual beating time or beating strokes. Scrape bowl and spoon or beaters often.)

Measure sifted flour, baking powder, salt, and sugar into sifter. Place shortening in mixing bowl and stir just to soften. Sift in dry ingredients. Add ¾ cup of the milk and the flavorings. Mix until all flour is dampened. Then *beat 2 minutes* in mixer at a low speed or 300 vigorous strokes by hand. Add egg whites and remaining milk and *beat 1 minute* in mixer or 150 strokes by hand. Fold in cherries and nuts.

Baking. Pour batter into two round 8- or 9-inch layer pans which have been lined on bottoms with paper. Bake in moderate oven (350°F.) 25 to 30 minutes, or until done. Cool, then frost with seven-minute frosting. Garnish with plump maraschino cherries and twigs of pine branches.

Betty Crocker's CANDY CANE COOKIES

...SO DIFFERENT, YET SO EASY TO MAKE!

These fancy holiday gift cookies look wonderful, taste even better. And, they're simple to make, easy to shape. Just follow this recipe and be sure you use dependable Gold Medal—America's favorite flour.

Preheat oven to 375° (quick moderate).

Mix together thoroughly......
- 1 cup soft shortening (half butter)
- 1 cup sifted confectioners' sugar
- 1 egg
- 1 1/2 tsp. almond extract
- 1 tsp. vanilla

Sift together and stir in........
- 2 1/2 cups sifted GOLD MEDAL Flour
- *1 tsp. salt

Divide dough into halves.

Blend into one half...... 1/2 tsp. red food coloring

Roll 1 tsp. each color dough into a strip about 4-in. long. Place strips side by side, press lightly together and twist like rope. Place on ungreased cooky sheet. Curve top down to form handle of cane. Bake *about 9 minutes* (or until lightly browned) in *quick moderate oven* (375°). Remove with spatula from cooky sheet while warm and sprinkle with a mixture of *1/2 cup crushed peppermint candy* and *1/2 cup sugar. Makes about 4 dozen cookies.*

SUCCESS TIPS: 1. Smooth rolls can be made by rolling small strips back and forth on lightly floured, cloth-covered board. 2. Make complete cookies one at a time. If all the dough of one color is shaped first, the little rolls become too dry to twist.

*If you use GOLD MEDAL Self-Rising Flour (sold in parts of the South), omit salt.

Betty Crocker of General Mills— First Lady of Food

Gold Medal Flour

Baking Trivia

Q. Although Betty Crocker was created in 1921, she was not a real person. In what year was her first official portrait produced? The illustration is used in the Gold Medal Flour ad above.

A. 1936 by artist Neysa McMein

More *The Saturday Evening Post Covers*

The Saturday Evening Post covers were works of art, many illustrated by famous artists of the time, including Norman Rockwell. Most of the 1953 covers have been incorporated within the previous pages of this book; the few that were not are presented on the following pages for your enjoyment.

The Saturday Evening

POST

January 10, 1953 · 15¢

Commuting Through Red Germany:
I RIDE NIGHTMARE HIGHWAY
By James P. O'Donnell

WHO ELECTED EISENHOWER?
The Story Behind the Landslide

JOHN FALTER

The Saturday Evening

POST

January 17, 1953 · 15¢

Shanghai Escape:
I CAME BACK FROM
A RED DEATH CELL
By Robert T. Bryan, Jr.

I think with you, that nothing is of more importance for the public weal, than to form and train up youth in wisdom and virtue.---Wise and good men are, in my opinion, the *strength* of a state far more so than riches or arms.

Benj. Franklin 1750

The Saturday Evening

POST

March 28, 1953 – 15¢

How Americans Lose Their Shirts
in Caribbean Gambling Joints

**MY YEARS IN SOVIET GERMANY'S
CONCENTRATION CAMPS**
By Horst Zimmermann

The Saturday Evening

POST

May 2, 1953 – 15¢

**THE
CORONATION**
England's Greatest
Moment
By PAUL GALLICO

The Saturday Evening

POST

May 10, 1953 – 15¢

SID CAESAR:
TV Gives Him Nightmares

**THE AMAZING MANSION
OF HENRY FORD**
By Joe McCarthy

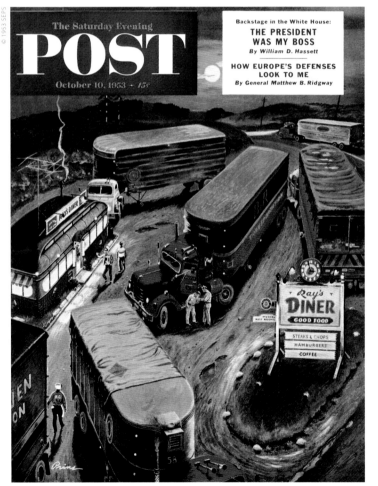

The Saturday Evening
POST
November 7, 1953 · 15¢

HOW EISENHOWER
PRODUCED
A FOREIGN POLICY
By DEMAREE BESS

© 1953 SEPS

The Saturday Evening
POST
December 12, 1953 · 15¢

Trapped by the Monsoon
Five Miles Up:
WE MET DEATH
ON K2

© 1953 SEPS

The Saturday Evening
POST
December 19, 1953 · 15¢

The Amazing True Adventures of
THE INCREDIBLE CAPTAIN KENEDY
By Richard Thruelsen

I Say Basketball's Our Best Game
By Coach Ken Loeffler

© 1953 SEPS

MORE FAMOUS BIRTHDAYS

January 5
George Tenet, former CIA Director, 1997–2004
Pamela Sue Martin, model, actress (Fallon Carrington of *Dynasty*)

January 6
Jett Williams, country musician
Malcolm Young, rhythm guitarist (AC/DC)

January 15
Randy White, NFL tackle (Dallas Cowboys)

January 19
Desi Arnaz Jr., actor

January 21
Paul Allen, co-founder of Microsoft

January 23
Pat Haden, NFL quarterback (Los Angeles Rams)
Robin Zander, musician (Cheap Trick)

February 2
Dog Chapman, TV personality (*The Bounty Hunter*)

February 5
John Beilein, basketball coach (University of Michigan)

February 7
Dan Quisenberry, baseball pitcher (Kansas City Royals)
Robert Brazile, NFL linebacker (Houston Oilers)

February 8
Mary Steenburgen, actress

February 9
Rick Wagoner, former CEO of General Motors, 2000–2009

February 12
Joanna Kerns, actress (Maggie Seaver of *Growing Pains*)

February 21
Christine Ebersole, actress (Maxie McDermott of *One Life to Live*)
William L. Petersen, actor (*CSI*)

February 22
Nigel Planer, actor (Neil of *The Young Ones*)

February 28
Ricky "The Dragon" Steamboat, professional wrestler

March 8
Jim Rice, baseball left fielder (Boston Red Sox)

March 10
Paul Haggis, screenwriter, film/TV producer, film director

March 16
Richard Stallman, computer programmer

March 25
Mary Gross, actress (*Saturday Night Live*)

March 26
Elaine Chao, former U.S. Secretary of Labor, 2001–2009

April 1
Barry Sonnenfeld, film director (*Men in Black*)

April 6
Andy Hertzfeld, computer programmer (co-founder of General Magic)

April 16
Peter Garrett, musician (Midnight Oil)

April 18
Rick Moranis, actor (*Honey I Shrunk the Kids*)

April 23
James Russo, actor

April 26
Nancy Lenehan, actress (Kay Hickey of *My Name is Earl*)

May 6
Lynn Whitfield, actress (Paula Van Doren of *Without a Trace*)
Tony Blair, former UK Prime Minister, 1997–2007

May 8
Alex Van Halen, drummer (Van Halen)

May 10
Jim Zorn, football coach (Washington Redskins)

May 15
Cleavant Derricks, actor (Rembrandt Brown of *Sliders*)
Mike Oldfield, musician, composer (*Tubular Bells*)

May 16
Rick Rhoden, baseball pitcher (Los Angeles Dodgers, Pittsburgh Pirates)

May 28
Jeff Bower, football coach (Southern Miss., 1990–2007)

May 29
Danny Elfman, musician, actor

June 1
Diana Canova, actress (Corinne Tate of *Soap*)

June 2
Craig Stadler, PGA golfer

June 5
Kathleen Kennedy, film/TV producer

June 11
Peter Bergman, actor (Jack Abbott of *The Young and the Restless*)

June 23
Russell Mulcahy, film director

June 29
Don Dokken, singer (Dokken)

July 2
Tony Armas, baseball outfielder (Boston Red Sox)

July 8
Anna Quindlen, columnist, novelist

July 11
Mindy Sterling, actress (Frau Farbissina of *Austin Powers*)

July 19
Howard Schultz, CEO of Starbucks

July 20
Thomas Friedman, journalist (*New York Times*)

July 29
Geddy Lee, bassist (Rush)

July 31
James Read, actor (*North & South*)

August 1
Howard Kurtz, media critic
Robert Cray, guitarist (The Robert Cray Band)

August 2
Butch Patrick, actor (Eddie of *The Munsters*)

August 8
Donny Most, actor (Ralph Malph of *Happy Days*)

August 14
James Horner, composer (scored *Titanic*)
Tom DiCillo, film director (*Living in Oblivion*)

August 20
Peter Horton, actor (Prof. Gary Shepherd of *thirtysomething*)

August 27
Alex Lifeson, guitarist (Rush)

August 30
Robert Parish, NBA forward (Boston Celtics)

August 31
Marcia Clark, attorney (former O.J. prosecutor)

September 6
Anne Lockhart, actress (Lt. Sheba of *Battlestar Galactica*)
Katherine Cannon, actress (Felice Martin of *Beverly Hills, 90210*)

September 11
Tommy Shaw, musician (Styx, Damn Yankees)

September 16
Christopher Rich, actor (Brock Hart of *Reba*)
Lenny Clarke, actor (Uncle Teddy of *Rescue Me*)

September 17
Rita Rudner, comic, author

September 21
Arie Luyendyk, auto racer (Indianapolis 500 winner, 1990 and 1997)

September 27
Greg Ham, musician (Men at Work)

September 29
Drake Hogestyn, actor (John Black of *Days of Our Lives*)

October 11
David Morse, actor (Mike Olshansky of *Hack*)

October 13
Pat Day, jockey

October 14
Greg Evigan, actor (*B.J. and the Bear*)

October 15
Larry Miller, comic, actor (Edwin Poole of *Boston Legal*)
Tito Jackson, musician (The Jackson 5)

October 20
Bill Nunn, actor (Terrence Phillips of *The Job*)

October 26
Keith Strickland, musician (B-52s)

October 27
Peter Firth, actor
Robert Picardo, actor (Holographic doctor of *Star Trek: Voyager*)

October 29
Denis Potvin, NHL hockey player (New York Islanders)

November 3
Kate Capshaw, actress

November 6
John Candelaria, baseball pitcher (Pittsburgh Pirates, California Angels)
Ron Underwood, film director

November 11
Andy Partridge, musician (XTC)

November 13
Frances Conroy, actress (Ruth Fisher of *Six Feet Under*)
Tracy Scoggins, actress (Grace of *Dante's Cove*)

November 18
Alan Moore, author (created *The Watchmen*)
Kevin Nealon, comic (*Saturday Night Live*)

November 19
Robert Beltran, actor (Chakotay of *Star Trek: Voyager*)

November 27
Curtis Armstrong, actor (*Revenge of the Nerds*)

November 30
June Pointer, musician (*The Pointer Sisters*)

December 2
Richard Jenkins, actor (Nathaniel Fisher of *Six Feet Under*)

December 6
Tom Hulce, actor (*Amadeus*)

December 11
Bess Armstrong, actress

December 13
Jim Davidson, comic (*Stand Up Jim Davidson*)

December 17
Bill Pullman, actor (*While You Were Sleeping*)

December 22
Bern Nadette Stanis, actress (Thelma of *Good Times*)

December 24
Timothy Carhart, actor (Eddie Willows of *CSI*)

December 28
James Foley, film director

Facts and Figures of 1953

President of the U.S.
Dwight D. Eisenhower
Vice President of the U.S.
Richard M. Nixon

Population of the U.S.
160,184,000

Births
3,902,000

College Graduates
Males: 187,000
Females: 105,000

Average salary for full-time employee: $3,853
Minimum wage (per hour): $0.75
Unemployment rate: 2.9%
Rate of inflation: 0.82%

© LIBRARY OF CONGRESS, PRINTS AND PHOTOGRAPHS DIVISION, FSA 3C04961U

Average cost for:

Bread (lb.) $0.16

Bacon (lb.) $0.79

Butter (lb.) $0.79

Eggs (doz.) $0.70

Milk (½ gal.) $0.47

Potatoes (10 lbs.)................$0.54

Coffee (lb.) $0.89

Sugar (5 lbs.) $0.53

Gasoline (gal.)......................$0.20

Movie ticket $0.60

Postage stamp.....................$0.03

New home..........................$9,550

REPRINTED WITH THE PERMISSION OF CARRIER CORP.

© GETTY IMAGES

Notable Inventions and Firsts

February 18: Lucille Ball and Desi Arnaz sign a contract for $8 million to continue the *I Love Lucy Show* through 1955.

March 5: Former congresswoman Clare Boothe Luce becomes the first woman to represent the United States in a major diplomatic position when she becomes the ambassador to Italy.

April 1: An Act of Congress establishes the Department of Health, Education and Welfare.

May: Writer Ernest Hemingway wins a Pulitzer Prize for his book *The Old Man and the Sea*.

May 31: The first nuclear reactor solely for energy production, called the Submarine Thermal Reactor, is fired up near Idaho Falls, Idaho.

August 12: Ann Davison, of England, lands in Miami, Fla., and becomes the first woman to sail single-handedly across the Atlantic on her 23-foot boat.

October: The first commercial computer to use RAM (random access memory), the UNIVAC 1103, is introduced.

Sports Winners

NFL: Detroit Lions defeat Cleveland Browns
World Series: New York Yankees defeat Brooklyn Dodgers
Stanley Cup: Montreal Canadiens defeat Boston Bruins
The Masters: Ben Hogan
PGA Championship: Walter Burkemo
NBA: Minneapolis Lakers defeat New York Knicks

1953: Dow Chemical began marketing Saran Wrap as a household product used to cover dishes and wrap sandwiches.

1953: Norman Larsen, president and head chemist at the Rocket Chemical Co., developed WD-40, the rust- and corrosion-prevention product.

1953 Quiz Answers

1. "The Doggie in the Window," page 24
2. Jacqueline Cochran, page 54
3. *The Arthur Murray Party*, page 23
4. 444 precious jewels, page 39
5. *Gentlemen Prefer Blondes*, page 7
6. *Kukla, Fran and Ollie*, page 67
7. *I Love Lucy*, page 26
8. John F. Kennedy and Jacqueline Bouvier, page 77

NATIONAL BASEBALL HALL OF FAME LIBRARY COOPERSTOWN, N.Y.

Live It Again 1953

PROJECT EDITOR	Barb Sprunger
CREATIVE DIRECTOR	Brad Snow
COPYWRITER & RESEARCH ASSISTANT	Becky Sarasin
EDITORIAL ASSISTANT	Laurie Lehman
COPY SUPERVISOR	Deborah Morgan
PRODUCTION ARTIST SUPERVISOR	Erin Brandt
PRODUCTION ARTIST	Edith Teegarden
COPY EDITORS	Mary O'Donnell, Sam Schneider
PHOTOGRAPHY SUPERVISOR	Tammy Christian
NOSTALGIA EDITOR	Ken Tate
PUBLISHING SERVICES DIRECTOR	Brenda Gallmeyer

Printed in China
First Printing: 2012
Library of Congress Control Number: 2011938395

Customer Service
LiveItAgain.com
(800) 829-5865

1 2 3 4 5 6 7 8 9